FOREVER
ELEVEN

FOREVER ELEVEN

JERRY RAAF

PRIMIX
PUBLISHING
THE WRITE CHOICE

Primix Publishing
East Brunswick Office Evolution
1 Tower Center Boulevard, Ste 1510
East Brunswick, NJ 08816
www.primixpublishing.com
Phone: 1-800-538-5788

Published by Primix Publishing: 09/08/2025

ISBN: 979-8-89194-531-9(sc)
ISBN: 979-8-89194-532-6(e)

Library of Congress Control Number: 2025915098

CONTENTS

A **MUST READ**, guaranteed to make you laugh just after your breath has been tugged by the unbridled fear, youthful bravado and foolish dares of a naive adolescent. This would make a wonderful family movie; one that you would likely return to see several times. Excellent book for youth or adult.

Cam Gardner, Seattle, WA

I marveled that this young man survived so many adventures during his eight week summer vacation. The quiet moments between idiotic dares stretched him, allowing him 'to be' and made me long for the innocence of my youth. Each chapter teased my emotions and when I read the last chapter and the epilogue, I did not want the book to end. A wonderful true life story, yet seemingly dream-like in its telling.

L.I. Winthrope, Toronto, ON

A narrative of adventures as satisfying, as a freshly baked piece of chocolate cake to a chocoholic. Live in the young man's battles, his amour, the exhilarating experience with a bear and so much more. Wrap yourself in this wonderful picturesque book and become lost in the funniest and most heart warming story you will read in a long time.

J. Tug Lansdown, Calgary, AB

Many emotions ran through me as I read this book, and when I closed it, I felt an uneasy calm for I realized that the eleven year old was not the main character. I reread the book two days later to see if I could find out what his name was. This book touched me; making me envious for such a summer.

Sara Jane Melford, Vancouver, BC

A GIFT TO

_____

FROM

_____

DATE

_____

'Thank You'
Jim Robertson
For your encouragement and suggesting a title for this book.
Your verbal pat on the back gave me
courage to write this story.

OVERVIEW

How well I remember my first night at Aunt Mabel's Broken Antler Ranch on the eastern side of the Rocky Mountains in Western Canada. It was an adventure that an eleven-year old city lad, such as I, needed to prune pride and bravado from my character so that I could learn to appreciate the value of life and family members I knew little about. Aunt Mabel's life was an enigma that unraveled before me and left an indelible mark on my memory and reasoning. She was such an inspiration 'to be' which I will never forget, even in my old age. I gaze daily at her photograph which is attached to my dresser mirror.

Influential people walk among us, modeling strength, independence and tenacity. Their actions can alter our potential, encouraging us to travel down paths previously unknown and to savor unique opportunity otherwise lost by compliancy, fear and self doubt. Such models have the potential to sculpt us, to fashion us and to mold us, allowing us to motivate others. These people can affect our memory, reason and foresight, to better face the challenges and fears in uncertain futures.

My aunt was such a model. She convinced me to take risks and not to live out the expectations of others. This journey was far too important to remain huddled among the intimidated, the frightened and the ultra conservative. The challenge of facing uncalculated perils taught me to keep my eyes on horizons, yet undiscovered.

The freedom and encouragement she gave caused me to embrace opportunity and risk rather than living in the shadow of regret. The excitement of chance tugged at my breath and prompted my spirit to view choices as privileges.

The discovery of a new world filled with 'life and limb' events is still with me after these many years. It was a summer of excitement, of growing up, and of personal crisis, some of which I have yet to deal with. The challenges were electric and somewhere during that summer, I changed from an invincible city kid, into a young man who had learned to cherish everything given to me, but now I mourn for what has been taken from me.

This book is dedicated
to a special lady

- 'RAINIE' -

wife and companion

Thank You
for encouraging me to write
about this narrow 'slice' of
my youth.

THE STING OF SILENCE

The antique pendulum clock chimed twelve times as I reached for more covers to shield the chill from my shoulders. If it had not been for the short fatigued candle on the night table, darkness would have rushed into my room with silent, yet frightening speed and devoured everything in its path, including me.

Staring at the door, I couldn't help but notice the occasional finger of darkness silently reaching under the door whenever the fragile flame moved to one side of the candlewick. Aside from a tree branch or something scratching against the window, the room was as silent as a sepulcher at midnight. The sound often caused me to turn my head to view shadows scratching at the windowpane. I was sure that the shadows were leaves tethered to scrawny branches that swayed in the summer breeze, but I often doubted what I tried to tell myself.

Again the antique hall clock mechanically notified me that another half hour had passed and by now I was sure that I should not have accepted my aunt's invitation to come to her ranch to get away from the wiles of city life. How could this be relaxation? The sound of sirens, cars racing engines and young people laughing at midnight was what I was used to, not branches on windows and antique clocks mocking my courage.

Not realizing that absolute silence, sprinkled with strange sounds, would be more intimidating than the sirens, loud neighbors and racing engines from stolen vehicles, I closed my eyes, held my breath and rued my willingness to accept this invitation to go to a place that intimidated me with the charms of nature and total darkness.

The darkness is blacker in the country than any corner you could find in the noisy city where I lived. New mown hay, tilled soil and spread fertilizer tugged at your nostrils in a different way than exhaust fumes from old cars, or stale odors of grease from a hamburger stand at the end of the block, or cigarette smoke clinging to old unwashed sleeveless shirts worn by sweaty laborers on transit buses.

Again the clock in the hall monotonously made its mechanical edict. Accepting that my first nights sleep in this dark intimidating room would likely be difficult; I rolled over at the very moment that the flame on the candle disappeared. Darkness invaded my room with frightening speed. In silence, I tried to hold my breathing but my heartbeat seemed so deafening. Unsure of how long I had held my breath, I gasped into the feathered pillow. Some time in the night my fears faded into vivid dreams, frantic kicks and irregular breathing.

CHAPTER 1

A HARD DAYS JOURNEY

In the early hours of June 30th, my father backed the faded '53 Ford Custom off the driveway and we were off to meet cousins, aunts and uncles in the Central Alberta town of Three Hills. My mother made arrangements for us to meet Aunt Mabel so that I could travel and spend the summer on her ranch located on the eastern rim of the Rocky Mountains. Her ranch was known as 'The Broken Antler Ranch' which sounded as if it were something out of the Old West.

My brother Oswald and I had never been to her ranch but my parents often spoke about her and what her ranch was like. I met her several times when we visited other relatives. All I remembered about her was that she wasn't very tall and weighed very little. "A gentle wisp of a woman" is how my mother referred to her, and I knew that my mother held her in high regard, even though they seldom saw or spoke to each other. Aunt Mabel was my mother's eldest sister.

I had no idea what a summer this was going to be. It certainly was more than my imagination could create and I had no way of guessing that this summer would be a time of maturing to the issues and dangers of this world. How could a Grade 6 student of Connaught Elementary Grade School possibly guess what life on a ranch would be like with an aunt he knew little about?

For this vacation, my father had purchased a new baseball cap for me, and my mother, well she had carefully selected and purchased a pair of blue pants, a red silk shirt with white tassels across the chest, new runners and a black leather belt with a large shiny buckle. All of these treasures were apparently part of living on a ranch as a 'Cowboy'.

Oswald and I had vivid images of what a cowboy should be like, after all we had seen every western show on our black and white television purchased from Eaton's on Third Street. There was The Rifleman, Roy Rogers, Hop-Along Cassidy, Bat Masterson, Wyatt Earp and our favorite, Have Gun Will Travel. All of these cowboys had several things in common; they were tough enough to fight with anyone who got in their way, they were willing to take a risk and were always friendly and courteous to good people. Oh, and another thing, many of these heroes were easy to recognize because they always wore a cowboy hat.

I wasn't concerned about my next months needs since I assumed that my mother had packed all of my necessities. They had been carefully placed into a small blue suitcase which had been tossed, by my father, into the trunk of the Ford sedan. If something had been forgotten, it was far too late to return, for the sedan was now leaving the comfort of pavement for a noisy, dusty, gravel road that would soon join the main paved highway to the city of Calgary.

Behind, I left the comforts and familiarity of summer vacation in the city for the excitement of living on a ranch with an aunt that I barely knew. My mind raced to the swimming pool on Bell Street. I knew that hundreds of kids would have abandoned their bicycles on the lawn surrounding the pool and their memories of school days for the pleasure of trying to swim in a pool that was far too crowded for wading. In the air would be the sounds of lifeguard whistles, screaming girls, laughing boys and the unmistakable splash of someone being tossed into the deep-end of the pool.

As my father adjusted his sun visor, my mother reached for the dashboard radio and dialed the small red indicator to 1070, CHAT radio. The music had a country sound to it as Hank Snow was just ending one of his songs.

Between my brother and me sat Charlie, a lop-eared brown dog of questionable heritage. Charlie had been an addition to the family several years earlier, much to the apparent annoyance of my father. Charlie meant no harm and lived under the assumption that everyone accepted his wet nose, his continual shedding and his playful ways. He seemed to believe that the world was at his disposal and that he had an unquestionable right to be in this family.

"Dogs should be living on a farm and not in a city," my father would often say but we learned to ignore his comments because we suspected that he liked Charlie as much as we did but didn't want to admit it. On several occasions, we would see our father absent mindedly scratch Charlie's ears during the six o'clock evening news.

The day seemed so perfect. How could two boys and a dog have it any better? A summer breeze blew through a partially opened car window, music was playing on the radio and another year of school was officially over, and both Oswald and I had passed into the next grade.

About an hour out of the city, Oswald pointed to a large brown bag on the floor of the sedan. My first thought was that if mother did not want us to eat what was in it, then she shouldn't have left it within our gaze and grasp.

I nodded and smiled as Oswald reached into the bag and pulled out a wax paper wrapped sandwich. He carefully and skillfully began to open the wax paper while my parents listened to a Patsy Cline song on the radio. I watched as my mother opened her purse to look for something and knew that she was sufficiently distracted that she likely wouldn't see or hear us when we raided the family lunch bag.

A moment later, the first sandwich was unwrapped and we found that it was filled with salmon, lettuce and mayonnaise. Fearing that my mother would smell the salmon, Oswald and I opened the rear windows of the sedan as far as they would open to allow fresh air to flow through the car. Even Charlie enjoyed a part of that sandwich.

The second sandwich had strawberry jam and Velveeta cheese. The third sandwich was made of ham but after two bites, Oswald and I including Charlie, refused to eat more of it because of the hot mustard that was on it. My father loved hot mustard but I suspected that he wouldn't be willing to eat any of it if he knew who had taken the small bites out of it, so I tossed it out of the window.

Over the next half hour, three apples, two bananas, twelve cookies and a chocolate bar made their way into our stomachs. The consequences of eating all of the lunch never crossed our minds but we soon found out how angry mom would get when she found out. Fortunately Oswald pushed the empty bag under the front seat.

Near noon, my father asked mom if she had brought any lunch. She turned and leaned over the back of the front seat to look for the large bag of food, which Oswald and I had just emptied.

"I made a great lunch for us and I was sure that I had put it into the car before we left, but it looks as if it's not here," she said with a strange look on her face. "Did you boys see it?"

Oswald looked at me and I felt the pressure to answer. "Yah, I saw it in the house," I said as my mouth went dry. "You had it on the cupboard. Did you see it?" I asked Oswald.

"Yah it was on the cupboard," he mumbled, with his mouth partially full of cookies.

Father entered the conversation with, "I brought it out and placed it on the floor in the back seat. It's gotta be there."

Mother spotted the empty bag partially hidden under the front seat. You can imagine what happened when she found out that the family lunch had disappeared. She was very angry and for a moment my brother and I were convinced that she was going kill us and that they were going to leave our bodies in one of the ditches by the side of the road.

Swinging wildly and blindly at Oswald and me, she shouted, "You ate all of the lunch?" Fortunately, she did not land any fatal blows but when Charlie barked and Oswald and I accidentally bumped our heads together, she turned to face the front. I guess she felt that we had paid the price for eating all of the lunch.

"Well?" asked my father.

She folded her arms and replied, "There were about a dozen sandwiches in that bag, not to mention the fruit, cookies and some chocolate cake." She continued as she stared in anger out the side window of the family sedan.

My father was not impressed either but stopped at a gas station by the side of the highway where six large trucks were parked. To calm his anger, he paced around the vehicle several times. Subtle invitations for us to step out of the car were ignored for we knew that imminent danger existed if we did. After all, how much more difficult could discipline have been if dad had to drag us from the back seat of the car to give us a beating? We were fortunate, however, for he was a man who was able to control his temper and cooled off quickly but mom, she remained in the front seat for a long time before stepping from the car.

After several large breaths she said, "Let's eat in the trucker's cafe. Food must be good or the truckers wouldn't stop here," she continued as she reached into the car for her purse and then slammed the door.

My father closed his eyes and waved his pointer finger at us. "Yah, let's try it," he said as he started for the trucker's café.

Oswald and I knew that it would take several minutes for mom and dad to cool their anger so we let Charlie run around to wet several tires before we tied him to the bumper of the car. When we thought it was safe, we joined them in the green and white vinyl booth near the jukebox.

The food may have been good but Oswald and I did not feel like eating, so we decided to play with Charlie while our parents ate.

About 4 o'clock, we arrived at my Aunt Annie's house in the town of Three Hills. This is where we were scheduled to meet Aunt Mabel and it gave us a chance to visit other relatives and play with cousins our age.

About a half hour later Aunt Mabel arrived. She smiled as she came over to where all of us were playing. Each one of them spoke briefly with her before she turned to Oswald and me. She knelt to hug Oswald and then stood to put her arm around my shoulder.

"All of my nephews have been to my ranch, so this year it's your turn," she said to me as she looked at both of us. "One day it will be your turn," she said as she ruffled Oswald's hair. "Both of you look like your father and it's easy to see that you're brothers. I never had kids but when I see boys like you, I wish I would have had some."

My mother came out of the house to meet Aunt Mabel and after they hugged they walked hand-in-hand into my Aunt Annie's house. Aunt Annie was the second eldest of the three sisters.

Oswald and I remained outside to play with our cousins whom we had not seen for some time, and it was great to share their bicycles and toys. Charlie really enjoyed himself too. He spent the first twenty minutes chasing the neighbor's cat and digging in their neighbor's garden.

Shortly after supper, Aunt Mabel walked over to me. "I'm glad that you decided to come and stay with me on the ranch. You'll have a summer that you'll never forget. Go and get your suitcase and put it into my old Fargo truck outside. We leave in ten minutes."

My mother hugged me, my brother nudged me and my father handed me three dollars. Charlie was nowhere to be seen. A few moments earlier, we saw him in the neighbor's yard sitting under a tree looking up at the cat, so I was not able to hug him before we left.

"I don't want you to forget us. We'll be back at the end

of August to pick you up, so we'll be seeing you," my mother said as she sniffed and wiped several tears from her cheeks. Fortunately, mothers are able to forget and forgive misbehavior of kids, especially young boys.

Before I knew it, we were in the Fargo and driving down a gravel road to some mystical ranch in the mountains.

"You'll love the ranch," Aunt Mabel said as she shifted into high gear. "There are lots of animals and always things to do. There's a rodeo that we'll go to and maybe I can talk Cliff into bringing over his pinto pony for you to ride and who knows what all will happen over the next two months?"

She was right. Who could know all of the things that could happen to a growing city boy over the next sixty days?

We drove in silence after she asked me about my school, teachers and the church we attended. It had been a long day and I was becoming tired.

"This truck is neat," I said as I looked over the dashboard and out the back window to see wooden rails on the cargo box.

"It's a Dodge Fargo. It needs a muffler and could use some tires but it works well, and I like the way it looks. Well used if you know what I mean," she said. "By the way, why not lie over on the seat and have a sleep. You're probably tired by now. I'll wake you when we get to the ranch," she said in an assuring way.

A horn beeped loudly and I sat up. My heart started pounding when I realized that it was dark outside and we were near her ranch. I looked up as we passed under a large, log gatepost and saw the skull of an animal with an antler on one side. The other antler was very short and in that fleeting moment, I saw that it had been broken off.

"So that's why you call it the Broken Antler Ranch?" I said as I rubbed my eyes and tried to orient myself to the blackness outside.

"Yes," she said. "It's one of the things that I care about. The ranch is not that big but it's all mine. Hope you like it," she said as she stopped at the front of a log cabin.

The headlights shone onto the porch where a collie stood, wagging its tail. "That's Fritz. He's my boy. He loves me and I love him. If you pet him, he'll be your friend forever."

She grabbed a flashlight from the glove compartment and then shut off the headlights. It was dark. I mean black dark. When she turned on the flashlight we made our way up the steps onto the porch of the log cabin. The darkness was so strong that I thought I could touch it, if not smell it.

I followed her into the log cabin and stood still as she struck a match and lit a lantern. "There, that's better," she said as she adjusted the wick and light began to gain control of the room.

"You hungry?" she asked and I nodded my head, not realizing that in that dim light she would not be able to see my head nodding up and down.

"If not, I'll show you to your room but before I do you'd better take this flashlight and go outside and have a pee. I'm sure that you don't want to get up during the night."

"Ah ... yah. You mean pee outside?" I asked, rather embarrassed that she knew that I had to go.

"Sure. Just don't pee on my flowers in the front at the house. You'll be safe out there. After all, if you can live in the city with all those weird people, you can live out here."

I gently closed the screen door behind me and followed the light from the flashlight. I stopped by the truck and while I stood there, I looked up at the sky. I never knew so many stars existed and how bright they were. It was such an amazing sight that I almost forgot that I had to pee.

I returned to the steps of the porch and stopped to look up again at the stars. It was something that I don't remember ever seeing before. As I stood there, I remembered something that Miss Simons had taught us in our grade 5 Science class. The Big Dipper was so clear and the North Star, wow! Off to my right was the Milky Way. I remember thinking that if we could have seen this in the city, maybe some of us students would have paid more attention in class.

Aunt Mabel opened the screen door. "You OK?" she asked. "I was worried that a bear may have come by and grabbed you."

"A BEAR! You mean that ..."

"You're OK, so come in and I'll show you to your room."

She ruffled my hair and used her left arm to give me a gentle hug. "I'm so glad to have you here. All of the other nephews have enjoyed it here, so I expect that you will too."

"How come it's so dark outside?"

"The darkest sky always shows the brightest stars. You have to look at the stars and not the darkness," she said as I followed her down a short hallway and up several steps.

She lit a candle in my room and closed the door. I stood there, unsure of what to do next. Maybe I should sleep in my clothes, especially if there were bears out here. Eventually, I sat on the edge of the bed and stared at the flame on the candle.

Soon I became very sleepy and I decided to take off my new runners and crawl into bed. The silence and darkness were so strong that I was sure that if I reached out from under the covers, I could touch them.

A pendulum clock down the hall rang eleven times after which I wondered how anyone could sleep through such loud ringing. Looking at the window, I could see something scratching at the pane and then I regretted removing my runners before crawling into bed. Sleep must have eventually overtaken me, and the sound of the clock never bothered me.

The most unusual sound I had ever heard awakened me and I sat up in terror. It was a sound that I had never heard before. My room was now filled with sunshine that was shining on my blanket. Rubbing my eyes, I looked around the room and at that moment I heard the strange sound again. Rushing to the window of my second floor room, I noticed a large, brightly feathered bird in my aunt's yard and it was craning its neck to call again. The bird looked like the colorful bird on my cornflakes box at my home back in the city.

Tucking in my shirt, I sat on the edge of the bed and looked at the room that had, only hours ago, held me motionless in a bed. How could such blackness exist and how could it have held me so securely?

After a breakfast of cereal and toast, my aunt walked to the front door of the cabin and motioned for me to follow her. As she reached for her big brimmed hat, I swallowed the last few gulps of milk, which tasted rather weird. When we stepped onto the front porch I scratched Fritz's ears and then followed her as she carried a metal pail to a red building, located down the hill from the rest of the farm buildings. The footpath was narrow and well worn, and I was amazed to see so many colorful flowers on either side of the walkway. I was pleased that Fritz was following me. He seemed to like me and I momentarily remembered Charlie.

All around the buildings were hundreds of fir trees and I immediately noticed that the air was fresh and easy to breathe. I inhaled an extra long breath and then ran to catch up with

Aunt Mabel. When I caught up to her, I suddenly became aware of odors that were totally unfamiliar to me. After rubbing my nose several times, it became apparent to me that whatever was in or near that red building was a threat to human life.

Aunt Mabel opened a gate and said something to me but I was unable to focus on what she was saying because of the odor. I interrupted her, "Auntie Mabel. Are you sure that it is OK to breathe that horrible smell?"

She chuckled as she continued to walk toward the red building.

"Will that odor stunt my growth?" I asked.

She chuckled and tilted her head to one side, "Don't know; maybe."

The handle of the pail that she carried squeaked loudly as we approached the red building she called a barn. An animal made a long 'MOOOOOOOOOOOOO' sound from inside the building and I tried to imagine what awaited me.

As we entered the dark building, something brushed against my leg, and somewhat terrified, I felt an urge to pee my pants. When I discovered that it was a long tailed white and brown cat, I swallowed quickly and pinched my legs together. The thought, that wetting my pants in front of my aunt would be something that she would never let me forget, gave me incentive to hang on.

Entering a dark barn from bright sunshine has its dangers, especially if you are not sure what you will encounter or step into. Within seconds Aunt Mabel was out of sight and I panicked when the animal called, 'MOOOOOOOOOOOOOOOOO,' again.

How could I, an adolescent, who had lived in the city, belonged to the Elm Street Gang which raided gardens, let the air out of car tires and fought in alleys, allow myself to be so intimidated by a mere animal? Maybe it was the strange and horrible odor?

When my eyes became accustomed to the darkness, I saw Aunt Mabel tug repeatedly on four finger looking objects that hung below this spotted creature she called a cow. I became intrigued with the idea that this is where milk came from, and I instantly decided that drinking root beer was safer than drinking milk from cows that live in smelly barns.

As the milk squirted from those long things, cats began to purr nearby and occasionally Aunt Mabel would squirt milk in the direction of a cat, which sat on its hind legs and opened its mouth to drink.

When the bucket was almost full of milk, she moved away from the cow and carried the bucket to a small table near the door. Turning to me, she said, "Come and help me. I need you to climb that ladder into the hayloft and throw some hay down for the cow to eat. There is a fork up there. It should be stuck in the pile of hay and the straw."

"How will I know the difference?"

"The hay is kinda green and straw is yellow. Cows eat hay and the straw is used for them to lie on," she said as she poured some milk in a pan for the cats that pushed themselves into a tight circle for a drink.

The task of climbing into the attic of the barn was new to me. As my aunt called from below, I began to push small amounts of dead grass and stale smelling straw down the opening to where the cow stood. As it fell onto the head of the cow, I couldn't help but question how green hay and yellow straw, eaten by a brown cow, could create white milk especially in such a smelly place. I was convinced that, yes root beer was better for me than white or chocolate milk.

CHAPTER 2

THE FEATHERED HORDE

After an early lunch, I decided to walk around the ranch while Aunt Mabel cleaned the kitchen. As I stood on the porch, I noticed a small wire pen with small birds, so I decided to see what they were like.

Small feathered creatures, hundreds of them, cheeped loudly behind the wire fence. Peering through the wire, I suddenly felt as if I were the one being watched. Hundreds of small black eyes stared at me as if I were on trial. One by one, they began moving toward the wire fence between us and when I moved, they stopped and looked at me. As a group, they appeared to be fearless. All of them walked slowly and as they did they jerked their heads. When they stopped they tilted their heads from side to side to investigate who and what I was. They were certainly larger than my friend's budgie bird and their beaks were straight and not curved.

Poking my finger through a small hole in the wire, I tried

to touch one of them. Instead, five of them stepped closer. I wiggled my finger to test their courage and in an instant, one of them bit me. The thought that they could bite made me to jump back and yell from the pain, and when I did, all of them fled to the other side of the pen.

My first response to the sharp pain was to put my finger into my mouth. The moment my mouth felt my finger I panicked for I remembered what my Health Teacher said about germs. This nip from this small, feathered creature would likely infect me and either I would lose my finger or simply get sick and die. I immediately spit several times on the ground, hoping to rid myself of any diseases or germs.

I looked at my bruised finger and in my momentary anger climbed the fence to deal with the biting bird. It took only a few steps before I realized that my new runners were now covered with large gobs of bird poop. Each sole was caked with the mushy, grey deposit. As I raised each foot to view the accumulation of poop, I became aware that the feathered horde had me surrounded. Chirping loudly, they seemed to be laughing at me, almost taunting me. I kicked at the front row of them, lost my balance and fell backward. When I sat up, my arm and clothes were covered with bird poop. The feathered horde, which ran away when I fell, approached me again. It was time to leave. Unsure of what they could do in such large numbers, I ran for the wire fence.

After clearing the fence, I walked over to the large trough where the cows drank water and there I washed my arm, jacket, pants and runners. This process took longer than I had anticipated and fortunately the strong afternoon sun dried my clothes within the hour.

Determined to return and become a victor of this

confrontation, I approached the wire fence in slow deliberate steps, so as not to attract attention. Once by the wire, I raised my leg to climb over the fence but the wire creaked loudly, warning the horde that I was near. Again, they started to move toward me. Their heads jerked as they walked slowly and cautiously toward me.

Something that my uncle said to me, when I started attending an elementary school in the tough section of town, now became my motto and motive. "You're bigger than them. So, give'm hell. Don't back away. Win or make them carry you away, but don't give up," he told me with a smile that showed several large gaps where teeth had been. I often wondered if the missing teeth and two large scars on his face had anything to do with the advice he freely gave to me that day. Despite my uncle's scars, I was ready to deal with these birds. I must admit that his words did give me courage, for I was certainly bigger than any of them even though they clearly outnumbered me.

Moving cautiously toward them, I gained confidence when they started to retreat. NOW I was in control and I liked that. Victory would now come to me but when the cheeping horde divided and suddenly circled behind me my confidence suddenly faded. Turning to retreat, I was confronted by a very large bird with long colorful feathers on his tail and a big floppy red object on top of his head. He looked like the same bird that had awakened me this morning.

He cocked his head to one side and his dark eyes blinked. I couldn't believe his size. His feet had large yellow toes and long black claws or hooks. He started to move toward me in a rather disjointed style of walking, bobbing his head from side to side as he approached. I remember looking at him and wondering why he had no shoulders.

I stood perfectly still, with only the tail of my shirt flapping in the afternoon breeze. We stared at each other for some time and then I realized that I needed a plan of escape. To my left was a large building, to my right was a stack of hay and to my rear was a building where all of these little monsters slept. My choices were to stand still and hope the bird would leave, or to run at him, hoping to scare him off. Hopefully this would allow me to get a head start and clear the fence that I had climbed over when I entered this fighting arena.

My enemy moved silently forward and was now within kicking distance of me. It was time for me to use my two feet. Remembering that kicking at them on this slippery surface was suicide, not to mention messy, I decided to take a large step forward and shout at him in the hope that he would retreat.

The moment my foot hit the ground, he jumped up, flapped his wings and landed on my chest. Terror struck my heart. This was different than any fight I had been in at school or in the park. Kids my size were large enough to grab onto or punch, but this feathered foe was about to take me down.

Closing my eyes, I raised one hand to protect my face and swung wildly with the other fist, hoping to land a sucker punch. Stumbling backward, I fought to keep my balance which became my priority. Within seconds my foe was on the ground and posturing in front of me again. His neck stretched and he cocked his head to one side as he prepared for another attack. His wings were spread like an eagle and his feet scratched the ground. Before I realized it, there were two other large colored feathered foes standing near the fence and they appeared to have decided to join his winning team. I was now officially surrounded and outnumbered, and I suspected that they had no intentions of taking prisoners.

Trying to justify my second loss, I vowed to escape and return at a more opportune time. The feathered horde began to cheep loudly as they approached me. It was time to leave. Running on a solid non-slippery surface is easy but running on this footing was treacherous. Within a moment, I was near the fence and jumped. My body cleared the fence but my left leg didn't and I landed face first onto the gravel pathway. There was a brief moment when I thought the large fighting birds had tripped me and were about to attack my butt.

It took only a moment to scramble to my feet. I ran as fast as I could to the porch of the log cabin. Aunt Mabel looked rather puzzled when she opened the screen door and stepped out onto the porch.

"Where on earth have you been? You've got chicken shit all over your runners, your arms are all scratched and your chin is bloody. My God, Young'un'; you're a mess. Take those shoes off and then wash this porch. You city kids can survive living on the streets and in alleys but you can't survive on a farm. What's this generation coming to?" Her voice became higher pitched as she made her comments.

Repairing my pride was high on my list of priorities, but it certainly wasn't more important than cleaning the porch, my runners and my scratches. While I worked, I tried to recall what went wrong; after all, these feathered creatures were smaller than me, so how did I lose both battles?

The rest of the afternoon was spent on the porch, scraping old paint off the front step and veranda. My aunt called it "farmer's work." I have no idea how long I had been there but I knew that I was ready for something to eat.

When my aunt opened the screen door, she carried a serving tray with a pitcher of lemonade and a small plate of cookies.

The next half hour was enjoyable and the sting of my losses faded momentarily from my memory.

Some time later, my aunt came out of the house and motioned for me to follow her. We walked, in silence, down the path that led to the pen where the feathered horde lived. I slowed as we arrived at the gate; unsure of what would happen next or what she hoped to accomplish.

"We need to prepare supper," she said without looking back at me.

"Supper?" I repeated in a monotone mumble as the corners of my mouth turned upward.

Before entering the pen where the horde and I had battled twice, she reached for an object that hung on the fence. It was as long as she was tall and on one end was a wooden handle and the rest of it was made of stiff wire that had a noticeable hook on the far end.

"You're not going in there, are you?" I asked, unsure of what she would say.

"Certainly, I am. Watch and learn, son," she said in a confident tone.

She opened the gate and confidently moved toward one of the large feathered fighters. I was sure that she would be maimed, if not killed. My heart pounded so loudly that I could hear it in my ears.

When she was within a short distance of the fleeing birds, she used the long hook to catch one of them by the foot and it flapped its wings in an attempt to escape. She pulled the bird toward her, grabbed it by both legs and turned it upside down so that its head was only inches from the ground. It continued to flap its wings but she was in charge of this fight. There was a moment when I wondered if she was going to give this bird a beating for what he had done to me, and I secretly wondered if she knew of my losing battles with these birds.

She walked over to the gate, opened it, stepped outside and closed it. After hanging up her hook, she walked over to a large block of wood and placed the large birds head on the wooden block and grabbed an axe that was stuck in the wooden block. **BAM**! Its head was gone with one swing of the axe.

Unwilling to approach, I suddenly realized that my aunt was a hand-to-hand killer. I wondered if her neighbors or relatives knew that she could kill without conscience or regret. The beheaded bird made some wild dance in the grass and when it was no longer moving, she picked it up and carried it toward the house.

"Wow, what a victor," I said under my breath. Silently I wished that two schoolyard bullies, Ralph Mannery and Mike Montgomery, could see this. Maybe, just maybe, they would leave me alone.

Aunt Mabel left the feathered corpse on the grass in the shade of the house and returned some time later with a large pot of boiling water. After dunking the feathered victim into the water five times, she smiled and said, "That's how you do it, son. I'll expect you to do that before you leave this place."

I had a large lump in my throat. Unable to swallow, I tried to smile but what she saw on my face must have surprised her, for she nodded her head and chuckled.

Over the next half hour, she was brutal. She pulled off all of the feathers, cut off its legs and even removed its insides. The sight and smell made me rush around to the side of the building for some fresh air.

When I returned, she and her victim were both gone. I knew that she had entered the cabin because I heard the screen door closing. Before me lay the results of the killing, for there was blood on the grass and feathers strewn everywhere. How could she so confidently move in and kill without fear?

As I scratched Fritz's ear, she shouted from within the house. "Carry that bucket of hot water over to the garden and dump it by the trees. And," she continued, "by the way, clean up the feathers and put them into the burning barrel, over by the shed."

Once my tasks were completed, I climbed into the hammock and looked at my scratched arms. Shame made me cover my face with the uninjured arm. I must have fallen asleep for I awakened suddenly when she called, "Come for supper and be sure that you wash up. I don't want to see dirty hands at the table."

Halfway through supper, I realized that we were eating the victim. With a partially eaten drumstick in my hand, I looked at her. "Does Colonel Saunder's do this to make his finger-licking good food?"

"I suppose he does," she said as she smiled at me. "I suppose he does."

CHAPTER 3

THE HAT, THE FAIR AND THE RIDE

The ride to the Country Fair was uneventful, other than being noisy; after all, it was an old Fargo half-ton truck that needed a muffler. I spent much of my time thinking of ways that I could poke a hole in the muffler of my father's car so it would make the same sound. On a long downhill stretch of road, the Fargo backfired several times, causing a dozen or so cows in the distance to raise their tails and run into the trees. The rest of the time, Aunt Mabel asked me about mom and dad, school and other cousins who lived in Saskatchewan. After miles and miles of dusty roads with high grass on either side, I began to wonder where this Country Fair was. Occasionally bugs splattered against the windshield and left a sticky reminder of their demise. Nothing seemed to distract Aunt Mabel, who seemed to be deep in thought, so I said nothing.

Overhead, ducks flew in a V formation and several gophers stood on their hind legs in the middle of the road, quite unaware that their furry hides were in danger of being run over. A large hawk sat on a corner post and stared at us as we passed, and in the field we saw many brown and white cattle grazing on the long grasses. Off to my right, I could see another meadow with several horses and a scruffy donkey.

Suddenly we rounded a corner and I could see a Ferris Wheel in the distance. It was then that I wondered if Aunt Mabel would have enough money to help pay for several rides. Then I remembered the three dollars that my father had given me, so I reached into my pocket to check if all of it was there.

Arriving at the entrance gate to the Fair Grounds, my aunt reached for her purse and counted out the exact change for us to enter. Once inside the dusty grounds, she drove the truck to a long line-up of other vehicles and shut off the engine. Again it backfired and she smiled as she looked into the rearview mirror and adjusted her hat.

"If nobody saw us coming, they sure must have heard us now," she said as she reached for the door handle. "Well, what do you want to do for the next hour?" she asked as she looked off toward a tent with dozens of balloons tied to it.

"I'd like to go on the Ferris Wheel but I only have three dollars," I said in an apologetic yet hopeful tone.

"Well, here you go," she said as she handed me a two-dollar bill.

"Five dollars is a lot of money," I said as I turned the faded orange bill over in my hand.

"No need to spend it all. So bring back whatever you have left, yah hear? You've earned some of it for your hard work in the garden and scraping the steps of the house the other day."

"Yes, Ma'am," I said as I stepped from the truck and slammed the door.

"Meet me down by that flagpole in any hour. See that flagpole?" she asked as she pointed to the pole in the center of the compound. "Please be there in one hour so we can go to the rodeo. One hour. Do you hear?"

"OK." I agreed and quickly ran toward the Ferris Wheel.

After several rides, four hotdogs and two soft drinks, I ran to the flagpole. When I arrived, my aunt appeared angry but she didn't say much. I looked down at my wristwatch and realized that I was ten minutes late. My mother would have boxed my ears, but Aunt Mabel did nothing and said nothing.

Nearby was a tent with dozens of cowboy hats. Some with strings to go around your neck, some with tassels on the brim and some hats made of straw. When I looked at all of them, I wished that I had saved some of my money for a cowboy hat, after all I was living on a ranch and cowboys don't wear baseball caps.

"Which one do you like?" she asked as her right hand removed my New York Yankees baseball cap.

"Don't know," I said as I moved closer to one of the tables with many different hats on it.

A dark skinned man behind the counter reached up and lifted a red hat off the wall and placed it on my head. "Hows 'bout 'dis one?" he asked.

"Looks too much like a girl's hat to me," my aunt mumbled as she lifted it off my head and handed it back to the salesman.

"I like the white one in the upper corner," I said hoping that he would hear me.

"Eets too big fo' ya boy," the man said as he reached for a blue one. "Blue's fir boys, you know," he continued as he attempted to place it on my head.

As I drew back, my aunt looked at him, "Blue is for boys in

this country but in China, blue is for girls. He wants a white one, so find a white one."

The man tried to reach a white hat and accidentally knocked down a straw hat. "Howse bout dis one?" he asked as he held it up for me to see.

"He wants a white one, so find it, yah hear?" repeated my aunt, without looking at him.

"Here's a white one. Will dis be better?"" questioned the man as he handed it to my aunt.

"Yes, that's better," she responded as she turned to place it on my head.

She cocked her head from side to side and after a moment of silence said, "There that looks better." Moments later she tilted it slightly to one side.

I walked over to a mirror to look at myself as she paid for it. I never did find out how much it cost, but she appeared to be as proud of it as I was.

As we walked away, she turned and adjusted the hat to an even sharper tilt on my head. "There, that's better. Makes you look rather handsome," she said with a girlish grin.

"Did we leave my new baseball cap at the …?"

"No," she interrupted, "I put it into my purse."

After an ice cream cone, a soda, some licorice and another hot dog, we found ourselves next to a narrow booth that led to public seating. The lady selling tickets wore a large white cowboy hat, and for a moment I regretted choosing a white hat. Maybe it was a hat for a girl, I thought to myself. "Yuk," I muttered as I kicked the ground in disgust.

The lady in the booth handed me two tickets and Aunt Mabel and I walked through a turnstile, like the ones used at hockey games or movie theatres in the city. As we rounded the corner, I saw six men, all wearing white cowboy hats. Now I felt better. If they could wear white, so could I.

Pausing a moment, I tried to tilt my hat even more, to match how the cowboys wore theirs but it almost fell off so I put it back the way it was before. Just then my aunt touched my arm and pointed to the top of the stands where our seats were.

"This is usually a very good rodeo. You'll love it," she said as she looked at our tickets. "Much of the crowd is already in their seats, and we are over there in Section R, row Z and seat number 11 and 12.

"What happens here?" I asked, expecting to see an oval track for racing cars but instead there were men and women riding horses in a circle and some of them were carrying flags as they rode.

"This is a rodeo. Don't tell me you've never been to a rodeo?" asked Aunt Mabel as she sat on seat number 11.

"Rodeo? No. I've heard of them, but have never seen 'em. What happens?" I asked as I grabbed my hat which was about to fall off.

"Sit and watch," she said as she waved at a lady a few rows down from us.

For the next hour or two, I sat in silence as men and girls did daring things, like riding angry cows, calves, horses and sheep. I reckoned that this was a place where bravery was measured and boys become men and girls become … well, they become bigger girls.

Suddenly, my aunt and the crowd cheered but I just watched in silence. Two men with painted faces and colorful baggy pants suddenly appeared and waved at the crowd. I watched as they ran in front of a cow to keep it away from the rider who had just fallen off. These cows had large horns and looked dangerous. One of the angry cows ran into the man with the baggy pants and he flew through the air and over the wire fence. The crowd stood to their feet and became silent, until they saw him limping to a small gate near a shack. Then the crowd cheered and clapped their hands.

"What a brave guy! That's like getting hit by a car," I whispered to myself as I removed my hat for a better view.

All of my excitement was heightened by the sound of my aunt's voice. Her screaming and yelling brought goose bumps to my arms. At one point, she jumped to her feet and knocked off my white hat, but fortunately it did not fall between the seats to the ground far below.

I drank more soda pop and ate popcorn, chocolate and two more hotdogs. By the end of the two-hour rodeo, I felt sick to my stomach but I stayed in my seat. I was sure that these country people were tougher than the people I met at ballgames, in the parks and in alleys of the city.

As the rodeo finished, my aunt turned to me and said, "Did ya notice that the best rider of the horses and bulls were men with white hats? Now ain't that great? Did yah enjoy that?"

I hadn't noticed, but if she said it, I was willing to believe it. We stayed after the rodeo and walked along a wire fence that led us to where the wild cows and horses were kept. My aunt called these gates, chutes. "This is where the cowboys and cows started their ride," she said.

These chutes were really big and so were the cowboys who were standing around smoking 'roll your own' cigarettes. The only animals that I could see myself riding were the sheep 'cause that is what some of the young boys were riding. I figured since they were close to the ground, you wouldn't likely get hurt if you fell off. The only other animals that I would try to ride were baby cows, which I soon learned were called calves.

Somehow, walking between these men with their white hats made me feel tall and strong, just as they were.

"What kind of boots are they wearing? They have pointy toes and silver things on the heels that jingle, when they walk," I questioned naïvely.

"Those are spurs and the boots are called cowboy boots. They are pointy so they fit into the stirrup of the saddle and the pointed toe makes it easier to remove your foot if you get thrown off the horse. Come here and I'll show you," she said as she tugged at my arm.

I didn't want to leave this place. This was the best place in the world! It was better than sneaking into Freddie's Pool Hall on Balmoral Street or into a movie that showed pretty girls.

For the next two hours, I rode on every ride in the midway several times. Only one ride made me feel sick, mind you all those hot dogs, sodas, chocolate and other stuff probably contributed to my nausea. This was the most perfect day of my life.

As evening arrived, Aunt Mabel took me back to the seats we sat in during the rodeo rides because as she said, "There will be fireworks after the evening show. Life couldn't get any better."

Several groups of cowboys played guitars and sang, one man had trained dogs and a man stood on stilts and juggled white bottles of milk. I enjoyed it all but the fireworks were the best. The colors were wonderful and the loud bangs echoed out into the trees next to the rodeo grounds. Besides, no one could have fallen asleep with that noise.

I remembered walking back to the truck but didn't remember riding home. My aunt woke me and I staggered up the porch and into the house. There she removed my hat, handed it to me and sent me up the stairs to bed. The darkness didn't frighten me this time, 'cause I fell into bed and slept with all of my clothes on including my runners.

My dreams were about riding horses and bulls in front of a large crowd and my aunt as she was cheering. Hers was the loudest voice of all. I rode black ones, white ones and brown ones. I only fell off once and the bull chased me and then I woke up. My heart was pounding as I discovered that I was climbing over the footboard of my bed.

"Yoooohooo! Breakfast is ready. Yohooooooo!" Aunt Mabel called.

I jumped out of bed and the first thing that I did was check to see if I had wet the bed when the bull had chased me. With no wet spot found, I breathed a sigh of relief, grabbed my white hat, tucked in my shirt and started for the stairs.

"Did you like the rodeo, Young'un'?" she asked as I reached for a chair.

"Oh yah. If I could I'd ride one of them bulls," I managed to say with mouthful of cereal and a gulp of milk, "I'd be the best rider anyone had ever seen."

"You would like to ride the bulls? Hahahahahah!," was her reaction. "You might be able to ride one of the sheep or a calf but not those bulls. They weigh more than my Fargo truck and certainly move a lot faster." She clicked her tongue and poured herself another coffee as she wagged her head from side to side.

The last gulp of milk went down my throat, "Yah, I think I could. Nothing could stop me. I'd walk up to him with my spurs on and then ride for the crowd. After all, I have a white hat, don't I?"

"You need more than a white hat to stay on the back of one

of them bulls. You'd need glue on your pants and someone prayin' to keep yah alive."

"I know that I could do it. All I need is a chance. I'd show the crowd." I responded as I stood to show her my confidence.

"OK, OK. Just sit and finish your breakfast. Don't mean to be rude, but if a fighting rooster was able to beat you, then these animals would put you in the hospital if not the cemetery."

"But I … how did you know about … the rooster?" I asked, suddenly shaken that she knew about my confrontations and my defeats.

"Finish your breakfast, son," was all she said as she stirred her coffee.

After breakfast, I was asked to weed the front flower garden. This wasn't what a strong and daring cowboy should be doing, so why did I have to do it? A boring hour passed before my aunt appeared behind the screen door.

"Clean yourself up cowboy, 'cause we're goin' to town."

Moments later, I was washed and ready to go. She drove down the country lanes and we arrived in town but this time, we came to the rodeo grounds from a different road and it led to the rear side of the chutes.

"Sit here a bit, son. I'll be back," she said as she closed the door of the Fargo.

I watched her walk around to the front of the truck and disappeared into a small building. The noon sun was warm and I was excited to be back at the rodeo. I adjusted my hat and then removed it to see if it had any dirt on it. This was the best that money could buy.

Suddenly, I heard a crowd cheering and realized that there was a rodeo going on. I jumped from the truck and ran for the metal fence near a small wooden shack. People were cheering for a cowboy who was riding a bucking horse. It was then that I spotted the man with the colorful baggy pants and painted face. He was not out with the rider but he was walking past me only a few feet away. I felt my eyes widen. He was short, and limped when he walked, but that didn't matter 'cause I was sure that he was the bravest man I'd ever seen.

I wanted to call to him but my mouth suddenly went dry. I started to wave and he tipped his hat, winked at me and disappeared behind the chutes.

I heard my aunt's voice so I ran back to the Fargo. When my aunt met me she smiled, "So you think you can ride, do you, son? Well let's find out. Come with me," she said as she led me to a small wooden building.

Once inside the small shack, a tall man knelt down and in a deep voice said, "Howdy, Tex. You're aunt sez you've survived all kinds of city life and now yah wanna try country life. So you want to ride, do yah?"

My eyes tried to adjust to the light, and I stepped back to look at my aunt. Clutching her purse, she smiled and nodded her head up and down but said nothing.

"I was just …"

"I think your aunt is a special person too," he said as he stood and walked over to her. He whispered something in her ear and she smiled, then he turned to me and motioned as he started for the door, "Come with me, Tex."

There was a moment when I was not sure if this was a dream or a nightmare. He motioned to me again, so I followed like a sheep to the slaughter.

The horses were bucking and the metal gates were banging as the crowd cheered but I … I was following the tall man down a narrow hallway with fences on either side. He stopped and picked up a colorful pair of leather pants that had parts missing at the crotch.

"These are called chaps and they belong to my friend's son but he's not able to be here 'cause he hurt his leg riding sheep two days ago. I think your aunt is right. You should have a chance to ride. By the way, how old are you?"

"E - E - Eleven, sir," was all that came out of my mouth after which I tried to swallow.

"Well, you're too old for Mutton Bustin', so I guess you'll have to ride a calf."

"What's a mutton?"

"Mutton means sheep. You're too old to ride one of them, so you'll have to ride a calf. What do yah think of that?"

"M ... mutton? A calf?" I stammered as it became increasingly difficult to breathe.

"Come on Tex, let me help you," he said. With that he began to strap the colorful leather pants onto my legs. I was too surprised to say no. When he was finished, he adjusted my white hat and said, "Go show us how to do it, city boy. Here's a pair of leather gloves. The crowd will love ya. Trust me."

A surge of energy rushed into my eleven-year old body. I had a white hat, colorful leather pants and leather gloves. Most of all, there was a crowd waiting for me and I knew that my aunt would be watching. Who could ask for anything more?

We walked among tall cowboys wearing spurs and different colored hats. They all seemed so tough, yet they looked down at me and smiled. One actually gave me the thumbs up and another patted me on the back and said, "Good Luck."

Here I was one of them and I hadn't even finished school. "Wait 'til I tell my mother. She'll be proud of me, and my brother, well he won't believe me," I whispered to myself as we walked behind the chutes. My legs seemed wobbly and my knees felt like Jello, but I did my best to keep up with this tall man. Walking with the colorful leather pants was hard to do, 'cause I had never walked like that before. We stopped beside a small fenced off area where I received my riding instructions.

"We'll set you on the back of that red and white calf over there," he said as he pointed to his right. "Grab the rope with all your strength and then we'll open the gate. You're job is to ride like the wind, boy. RIDE. YAH HEAR?" Just then the crowd cheered again. I guess I appeared dazed so he asked again. "Do yah hear me, boy?"

"Ah yah, I guess so," I managed to whisper as I tried to swallow, but couldn't.

I happened to look through the metal fence and spotted Aunt Mabel near the fence quite some distance away. She was waving as she peered between the bars of the metal fence near the grandstand.

Just then the announcer began with, "Ladies and Gentlemen. This afternoon, we are having the young boys Wild Calf Riding Championship. This may look easy but remember that these calves have never been ridden before, but I think these young boys are tough enough to do just that. Let's encourage these young men, so let's give them a round of applause!"

The crowd cheered, my aunt waved and I had the sudden urge to go to the bathroom.

There was a pause and I felt my stomach churn, and then I heard the announcer say, "The first young man to attempt a ride may be a city boy, but this afternoon he is riding for Jessie Jenkins, who was hurt in the rodeo yesterday. This takes courage so let's hear it for this young city boy!"

He may have said my name but I didn't hear it, for the crowd was cheering. Now I knew that I had to go to the bathroom but there wasn't time.

"The prize money for this event," the announcer continued, "is a set of leather chaps and a pair of leather gloves, complements of McKay's Hardware and Albert's Grocery Store. Let's hear it again for these brave young men."

Somehow the word 'brave' seemed so out of place. I was about to crawl over the fence and throw up but the tall man grabbed me and started to lift me up, so I climbed up the metal fence and looked down. There he was; a red and white calf but boy did he look big. The man nudged me so I climbed onto the back of the wild beast.

As the crowd cheered, I felt the two strong hands lower me onto the back of a red and white calf. It breathed uneasily and then made a loud "**MOOOOOOOOOO**" sound. It bobbed its head from side to side and I felt my legs shake as its rib cage breathed under me. My bony butt felt every bone in its spine. For a moment, I remember thinking, "So this is what it's like to die."

As I grabbed the rope that was around the chest of the calf, someone pushed my new white hat down over my ears and half way over my eyes. Suddenly the gate opened and there was a wide-open space in front of me. The calf started to run and it passed the man with the painted face and colorful baggy pants.

Everything seemed like a blur; kinda like riding on one of the Fair Ground rides. The calf turned in front of the crowd, jumped, mooooooed, huffed and puffed, bobbed its head and stumbled. I heard a couple of loud farts and wondered if it was me or the calf.

Suddenly my life slowed down to almost a stand still. Dirt flew up into my face, the crowd cheered and I thought I heard my aunt screaming. Then my face hit the soft dirt and all of my bones seemed to come apart. I could not see for the dirt in my eyes and suddenly the beast was back up on its feet and running, and I, yes I was still riding. The crowd cheered again and again. I thought I heard Aunt Mabel yelling but I had no idea where she was. I heard a loud horn sound and then I heard someone yell, "**LET GO OF THE ROPE, SON, AND JUMP!**"

Again, the calf and I went around the open space and out of the corner of my dirt filled eyes I could see a bunch of cowboys trying to catch the calf. It ran over two men and continued to run in a wild rage. I hung on, for my life was on the line. Suddenly I felt some wet slime hit my cheek and I guess it was saliva from the calf.

Through the open area we went again, and this time the calf stumbled from exhaustion and fell to its knees. It was still huffing and puffing but too tired to continue. Someone grabbed me and shouted, "Let go of the damn rope, boy or you'll ride him to his death!"

I rubbed the dirt from my eyes and I looked up at the crowd that was still cheering. Frozen by the applause, I stood on trembling legs until someone grabbed me and carried me to a side gate. There someone handed me a gray crumpled cowboy hat.

"I think this is yours," the unfamiliar voice said.

"That's not my hat. Mine was white," I whispered in a quivering voice.

Someone hugged me. I rubbed my eyes to see who it was and recognized Aunt Mabel. She seemed so happy that she was crying. "Son, first I thought you would die and then …" she gasped, "then I thought I would die but … but after a few minutes, I was sure that the calf would die."

"But my hat," I said as I bent over to spit dirt from my mouth.

For the next twenty minutes, I watched the other young boys try to ride calves, all but two fell off. Then the announcer called my name, and my aunt told me that I had won the contest! My prize was a pair of blue and white leather chaps and a pair of leather gloves with snaps on the cuffs.

My aunt cried all the way home. And I, well I sat in the back of the old Fargo and continued to spit dirt from my mouth and shake the dust from my hair.

Was it worth it? Well, the chaps were mine and so were the gloves. Now, I was a real 'Cowboy'. The only thing I felt bad about, was my white ... ah dirty hat.

Wait until Oswald and dad hear about this.

CHAPTER 4

THE BLACK YEARLING BULL

How could an eleven year of boy, with a soiled hat, new blue and white leather chaps, black leather gloves and a perfect riding career, possibly ignore his new-found talent and hide his potential? If being a cowboy meant that a rider rode cows then it made perfect sense that what I was … only a calfboy, for riding a calf.

Somehow this didn't have the same ring to it, as 'Cowboy.' This meant that the next thing I had to do was to ride a cow or a bull, like the grown men did. This move to the next level seemed so logical. All that I needed was opportunity. If none presented itself, perhaps it was time to create one.

For three days, my thoughts were concentrated on how I could get a chance to ride a cow, male or female. An opportunity certainly was not created in hoeing the garden, painting the fence, cutting grass with a push-mower or cleaning out the barn. The only thing that could take my mind off my riding career was my aunt's cooking. A growing boy needs good food and lots of it.

Opportunity happened while I was cleaning the loft of the barn. I heard a noise on the ground floor and peered down the ladder hole. There to my surprise was a black male cow, which I remember my aunt calling a bull. She told me that it was a one year old and so she called it a 'yearling'. She said that his kind was known as an Aberdeen Angus.

I stood in silence and looked down at the black bull as he ate food out of the manger. He appeared to be quite tame and disinterested in his environment. Aunt Mabel did say that he came from good stock, but was a bit nasty. As I watched, he turned and started to walk out of the barn. A moment later, I climbed down the wooden ladder to watch as he stepped into the afternoon sun. His black skin shone in the sunshine. He had fat wrinkles around his neck, and his yellow horns were small but intimidating. His muscles rippled as he walked and he swished his tail as if he knew I was watching him.

For the next two days, I looked for a place where I could pen him and get on his back. I couldn't stop thinking about it. My desire to ride him increased, especially when I played with my chaps. Every time he stopped at the water tank for a drink, I approached him for a better look.

One of those times, he looked at me, lifted his nose to sniff the air, snorted, shook his head and walked away, leaving me more determined than ever to ride him. He might be bigger than the calf I had ridden and he might be more difficult to ride, but how could I know unless I tried?

Late Thursday afternoon, an old red pickup truck came to the Broken Antler Ranch. Behind it, there was a large narrow metal pen on wheels which had lotza dried cow manure on it.

After shutting off the engine, the driver stepped from the truck, tipped his hat at me and closed the door. It was then that I recognized him. He was the man that my aunt had spoken to just before my calf ridin' experience at the rodeo. Calling out to him, I ran to meet him.

"Howdy Tex. It's nice to see yah again. By the way, my name is Cliff. That was some ride you put on at the rodeo. Hard to believe that it was your first ride," he said as he looked down at me. Moments later, he leaned against the fender of the truck, "The chaps you won are nice. What'ya think of them?"

I pulled down the brim of my hat, shuffled my feet and replied, "Yah and I think I could do it again if I had the chance." I held out my hand and we shook hands. Then I felt a little foolish, because I had forgotten to take off my gloves.

"You're a natural rider, son. I suspect that you're getting' ready for a career as a professional cowboy," he said as he reached into his shirt pocket for his pipe.

I pulled up my pants and spit on the ground. "Yah, I'd like to use my new chaps to ride somethin' bigger. Calves are good but they're kinda small, yah know."

Tipping back his hat, he looked toward the house and saw my aunt, who was standing on the porch of the house.

"Any more rodeos comin' up?" I asked but he didn't answer because he seemed distracted by my aunt. He put his pipe back in his pocket, grabbed a large can of coffee that was on the front seat of the truck and started for the house. I followed at a distance.

When he arrived at the house, he handed the coffee to Aunt Mabel. As they spoke I walked back to the barn to finish my chores. About half an hour later, I heard the sound of his truck beside the barn. Immediately, I climbed down from the loft and went outside. There, to my surprise, was Cliff backing his truck, with the large narrow metal pen attached to it, up to the fence next to the barn.

"What's that?" I asked Aunt Mabel as Cliff put the truck in reverse.

"It's a Squeeze Pen. We use it to treat animals with medicine, cut off their horns or neuter the calves," she said as she waved her hand to direct Cliff as he continued to back up to the side of the barn.

As Cliff unhitched the Squeeze Pen, she opened the rear gate. "That's where you have the cow or calf step into, and then we close the gate. When you want the cow to leave, then you just open the front gate."

"Quick and easy to use. Just remember to stay out of the way of the critter leavin' by the front gate," Cliff said as he tapped the cold ashes from his pipe.

"Kinda like the rodeo," I said as both he and my aunt walked back to the open door of the truck. I couldn't believe my luck for this was perfect for my riding career. Now all I needed was for Aunt Mabel to help me lure the black bull into the Squeeze Pen, so I could ride him.

Cliff stayed for supper and then I decided that maybe, just maybe, he was the one to help me. I needed to wait for the right moment to ask for his help.

While my aunt cleared the table, he and I stepped onto the porch. He lit his pipe and I sat on the handrail. The moon was rising in the east and I heard a loon in the distance.

"Cliff."

"Yah." he grunted as smoke flowed from his nostrils. He looked so tough and ready for rodeoing.

"Since I have been, I mean, I am interested in riding again, I would like ..."

"Yah want to ride again, do yah?" he asked as he stirred the ashes in the pipe.

"I want to ride again but this time I would like to try something bigger than a calf and ah, ah ..."

"Bigger? Well ... I don't recommend anything bigger," said Cliff as he drew smoke from his pipe. Smoke curled again from his lips and nostrils. "Calves are tough enough. 'Sides they're closer to the ground in case you fall off."

"Fall off! Oh, no I don't plan on fallin' off," I said with a tone of overconfidence.

He puffed on his pipe for a moment and then stirred the ashes in the bowl again. "No one plans on fallin' off or even gettin' hurt. None of us ever plans to do things that will fail, but sometimes life hands yah a sour apple. You may throw it away after you've tasted it, but the taste will still be in your mouth for a long time."

Aunt Mabel closed the screen door and sat on the swing, and for some reason I felt the need to go for a walk and leave them alone.

The next morning, my aunt told me that she was going to see a neighbor, who needed help because she had a new baby. Aunt Mabel knew that I didn't want to go along, so she didn't ask. Instead, she asked me to feed the chickens, hoe the last few rows of potatoes and paint the fence around the garden. What a way to have a fun day.

Her last words, before she closed the door of the Fargo, were, "I'll be back about 4 o'clock. Food's in the kitchen when you're hungry. See you in a few hours." Soon the faded Fargo disappeared behind the row of trees that lined the lane that led to and from the ranch.

Running up the stairs to my room, I began to plan how I could herd the black yearling into the narrow pen. In moments, I had my chaps, my gloves and my soiled hat, and was running down the wooden stairs toward the porch. When I was on the porch, I put on all of my riding gear, including my leather gloves. Now I was ready for the ride of my life. I ran across the yard with Fritz, the Collie, by my side.

Standing beside the Squeeze Pen, I looked out toward the pasture, hoping to see the black yearling bull. Off in the distance, I could see the herd of cattle grazing, so I eagerly started in their direction, knowing that the bull would be near them.

When I neared the herd, some of the cows that were lying down stood to their feet while some of the calves lifted their tails and started to run away from Fritz, who started chasing them. The black yearling walked toward me and began to paw the ground with his front feet. Dirt flew into the air and landed on his back. Small puffs of dust began to swirl around, carried by the soft summer breezes. He seemed to become more agitated by the moment for he was bobbing his head up and down as he snorted. Fear never entered my mind for I was wearing my leather chaps and was a champion rider; not some inexperienced kid who would be easily scared off.

Confidently, I moved toward the herd and circled them so that I could walk them back toward the barn. The only reluctant member was my future opponent, for he looked at me for some time before moving on with the herd.

An uneasy feeling came over me, for I felt that he suspected what was about to happen and did not like the idea that I could be in charge. Everything seemed to go as planned until it occurred to me that I had two problems; how could I get the right member of the herd into the Squeeze Pen and who would open the gate when I was ready to ride?

Once the cattle were in the corral at the front of the barn, I closed the gate behind me. I decided that the first thing I needed to do was to isolate the black bull from the herd and then gently chase him to the entrance of the Squeeze Pen.

Isolating him took longer that I had expected. By that time, I was tired and breathing harder than the time I had run a marathon at a school sports day. While I was catching my breath, he turned to look at me. Again, he pawed the ground and moved his head from side to side. Long strings of snot were hanging from his nose and he appeared to be rather upset. That is when I noticed that Fritz had moved outside the fence to watch me.

Suddenly, the bull started walking toward me with his head down. I was sure that he would stop. After all, I was a cowboy wearing chaps, gloves and a soiled hat.

Seconds later, a thought struck me with the speed of lightning crossing the evening sky; bulls at the rodeo chased the clowns who wore painted faces and colorful pants, so why not me? I remembered one cowboy at the rodeo being tossed over the fence and getting hurt. This was the first time that riding the bull didn't seem to be too smart.

By the time I came to my senses, it was almost too late. Fortunately, my rodeo instincts kicked in, so I turned and ran, my chaps flapping so awkwardly that I almost fell down. Ahead of me was the Squeeze Pen. As I stumbled to the entrance, I felt something nudge me. I pulled myself into the squeeze pen and moved as far to the front of it and climbed up the side of it. When I reached the top, I looked behind me to see where the angry black beast was. There he was standing with his head in the entrance of the Squeeze Pen. The strings of snot continued to spray from his nose as he shook his head and snorted loudly.

My heart was pounding so loudly that I was sure he could hear it. At that most inappropriate moment, my hat fell to the floor of the Squeeze Pen.

This was the moment for a decision. I was about to step down into the Squeeze Pen to get my hat when I heard Cliff's voice. "So, yah want to ride him, do yah?"

Without taking my eyes off the black yearling, I wheezed, "Yaaaaah."

"Well, let me help yah," he said as he climbed over the fence. "Climb down into the Squeeze Pen, Young'un', and when he charges you, climb like hell and don't look back. I'll close the gate."

I lowered myself into the Squeeze Pen as my four footed foe glared at me. He pawed the ground and slowly stepped forward. At that moment, Cliff struck him on the rump with a large wooden stick. He jumped into the Squeeze Pen and I climbed like hell. When I reached the top, I heard the steel gate slam shut.

"There you are son!" shouted Cliff. "Here's your chance to be a rider," he said as he wiped his mouth with the back of his hand.

The black foe tried to back up and when he was unable to he charged forward, moving the squeeze pen about two feet forward. I gripped the rail so that I would not fall off, and at the moment, he smashed his head on the sides of the squeeze pen and looked up at me.

Climbing down the outside of the Squeeze Pen, I looked at the large dark unblinking eye that was staring at me. The caged beast bobbed his head and bellowed.

'**MOOOOOOOOOOOOAAAAAAHHHH.**' His breath was hot and for the first time I knew what anger smelled like. My heart almost stopped and I jumped back from the side of the Squeeze Pen.

"This is tougher than I thought," I said as I stepped back a few paces, on my wobbly legs.

"You sure you're up to this?" Cliff asked as he placed his hand on my shaking shoulder.

Before answering, I looked back at the dark dilated eyes of the beast. The yearling seemed to dare me to try riding him. He seemed to want a chance to show me what riding was all about.

"He'll be tougher than you expect but he is young and young bulls generally run in a straight line. The experienced ones will turn, swivel and change direction but him, well … he's young," said Cliff with confidence.

"I … I don't know," I stammered and swallowed loudly.

"Well, you're faster than him. I saw you run," said Cliff as he pulled his pipe from his shirt pocket and then searched for a match.

One of my legs stopped wobbling and I dropped to one knee.

"You OK?" asked Cliff. There was a long silence and then he continued. "You don't have to ride him, 'cause I need him in this pen to check his health, brand him and take off his horns. No one needs to know that you didn't ride him."

I felt nauseated.

"It's your decision." Cliff walked over to the fence and opened the truck door. He returned with a small box and placed it on the ground next to the Squeeze Pen. Inside the box were needles and small bottles of medicine, along with other veterinarian tools and dressings. For the next half hour, Cliff examined the caged bull. He placed a branding iron on the yearling's hip and the smell of burning hair made me turn away for fresh air. Then, he put a rope around his neck to hold his head as still as possible. He proceeded to cut off both horns and blood began to squirt from the head of the humiliated animal. His heartbeat sent the blood shooting into the air and that is when fear gripped me for I was afraid that he would die.

The nausea was more than I could deal with so I leaned over the fence and closed my eyes. When I returned, Cliff had a long piece of twine wrapped around the small stumps, where the horns had been. The twine was placed in a figure eight around the horn stumps and when Cliff pulled on the twine, the bleeding suddenly stopped.

"Wow! Will that keep him from bleeding to death?" I asked, hoping he would say yes.

"Yes, I learned that from an old veterinarian in the Delbourne Three Hills area. His name was Dr. Bohay. It works like a damn," Cliff said as he used a towel to wipe the blood from the yearling's face. "Done," he said as he tossed the towel over the fence. It landed in front of Aunt Mabel.

"I see that you have a real cowboy helpin' you, this year," she said with a smile.

"Brave, good and tough, like you'd expect," Cliff said with a smile. He winked at me and I tried to smile.

"Well, for a moment, I was afraid that Cliff was helpin' you to ride the black yearling," she said. "He's a might tougher than the calf you mastered at the rodeo the other day," she continued as she leaned against Cliff's truck.

Cliff looked at me and then put more tobacco into his pipe. As he tapped the tobacco into place, he turned to look at Aunt Mabel, "Naw, he's just dressed as a workin' cowboy, and doing a good job, I might say."

She smiled as though she were relieved.

"No sense ridin' an injured bull. I ... I mean we just branded and dehorned him. 'Sides, he's in pretty rough shape and needs a day of two to recover."

I smiled and spit on the ground.

"Well Mabel, workin' cowboys need food to survive. Any of that apple pie left?" With that said, he opened the front gate and the bruised yearling sprinted for freedom.

While Cliff and I waited for Aunt Mabel to bring the pie to the porch after supper, he looked at me as the smoke flowed from his nostrils. "Next time you try to do something as important as testing your courage: have a friend nearby. Everyone needs some encouragement and help to make their dreams come true. It's wise to have someone nearby, especially on the dangerous dreams."

I ate my aunt's pie without taking off my chaps.

CHAPTER 5

DONUT, THE SHETLAND PONY

One morning Aunt Mabel told me that we were going into town to pick up the mail and buy some 'grub', which I found out later, meant food. After breakfast, we left for town in the noisy old Fargo. When we arrived, she parked in front of an unpainted building, Frank's Bott & Shue Repare Shopp. I remember smiling at the sign and felt proud that I knew how to spell boot, shoe and repair.

The passenger door of the Fargo needed repair because I had to slam it three times to close it. I followed Aunt Mabel up the rickety stairs to the veranda and then into the store. A bell rang when we opened the door and a rather scruffy unshaven man stepped from behind a tattered curtain at the rear of the store.

"Howdee, Mabel. Goot to say you agin. Vat can I git fir ya?" the old man said as he brushed his gray hair to the side with his crooked and brown stained fingers. It seemed to be a feeble attempt to appear more presentable. His large mustache covered his lips and it definitely needed washing and trimming. The leather apron that he wore was heavily stained and for a man who fixed and sold boots and shoes, he needed to replace his own shoes. I could see several small holes on the top of each shoe and the left one, had a hole so large that I could see that he wore no socks.

"Well, Lazlo," my aunt said as she walked over to the shelf of cowboy boots, "My nephew needs some cowboy boots."

"Vhat size unt coalor? Der are manny sizes." He lowered his gaze and looked down at my feet. "Vhat size are doze … canvas shoes?"

Before I could answer, my aunt handed him a black cowboy boot. "Let's see if this size will fit him."

He motioned for me to sit on an old wooden chair that had wire wrapped around the legs to hold it together. As I sat down, the chair creaked loudly. He smiled at me as he began to unlace my runners and I looked at my aunt to be sure that it was all right.

"Well, you can't go around wearing those nice chaps and have runners peeking out from under them, now can you? You need boots; cowboy boots," she said as she continued to look over seven shelves of boots.

A large grey cat walked silently across the counter and lay next to the cash register as Lazlo placed my foot into the tall black boot. "OK, now you kin stand yup and grrrabb dem here and pull dem on." He smiled and I could see more gaps than teeth.

My foot slipped into the new boot and it felt wonderful.

"What about the other boot?" I asked.

"Derr ya go, bouy," he replied. "Day is goot boots."

As I looked up at him, I noticed that his eyes were blue and they sparkled when he spoke. His face had many lines but they could not hide his friendliness.

"Do they feel good?" Aunt Mabel asked as she looked at me.

Unable to speak because of my surprise that my aunt would buy me boots, I just nodded.

"Walk around a bit and see if they rub on your heel or squeeze your toes."

I made several laps around the room before responding, "Their great."

We'll take 'em," she said as she opened her purse and moved to the cash register. As she paid for them, I opened the door and stepped out into the bright sunshine. Stepping off the veranda was difficult because I wasn't used to the high heel of the cowboy boot. I shuffled to the curb and as I stepped off, I started to wobble so I immediately grabbed the side of the Fargo. I didn't want to have anyone see me falling. Inside the truck, I looked down at the boots and wiggled both feet.

As Aunt Mabel stepped out of the door and called, "Thanks Lazlo. I wish you well."

When she closed the door of the truck, I looked over to her and said, "Thanks. I never thought I would ever get boots as nice as these. And thanks for my hat too."

"A boy … I mean a young man, needs boots, especially if he is workin' on a ranch. Runners are for silly city folk, who have nothing else to do but rush around and pretend they're busy. It may be style in the city but out here, well boots are best," she said as she started the engine.

"By the way, where are my runners?"

"They're in the back of the truck," she said as put the truck into reverse."

After picking up the mail and some grub at the grocery store, we started for home. As we pulled into the yard, I noticed Cliff's truck parked near the barn and I saw he was busy working near the squeeze gate.

I tried running over to see him but my new boots were too stiff and they didn't feel anything like my runners that Aunt Mabel had carelessly tossed into the back of the Fargo.

"Cliff! Cliff!" I called as I stumbled toward him. He leaned over the fence and tipped his hat back. "What in thunder's the matter, Young'un'?"

"Look at my new boots. Just got 'em. Kinda stiff, but Aunt Mabel says they'll be better in a few days."

"Yah gotta break 'em in. If you do, they'll feel great and be the best thing your feet could ever have."

"Break them in?" I asked, unsure of what he meant.

"Good boots are like a good horse. But before either of them is good, you gotta train them. Come with me, but yah gotta trust me. I wouldn't steer yah wrong. 'Sides if I ruined your new boots, Mabel ... I mean Aunt Mabel wouldn't be pleased with me."

Within minutes he poured several pails of water into a large metal container that was in the back of his truck. "It may be a bit cold but step in," he said.

I looked up at him as if he were crazy.

"I'm serious," he said as he smiled. "That's how all cowboys train their boots."

"But, I ... I didn't know that boots ..."

He interrupted. "Step into the water son and stay there for as long as you can." With that said, he walked back up to the Squeeze Pen and continued giving a needle to one of the cows.

After staring at the house for some time, I stepped into the cold water with my left foot. I really didn't believe him, but I decided that I would do what he said. I thought about it, if my boots were ruined I'd tell Aunt Mabel that he was the one who told me to do it. Eventually I put the other foot into the water.

About a half hour later, I sloshed my way over to where Cliff was working.

"So how are they?" he asked.

"My feet are cold and there's water in my boots. Now what do I do?" I asked in a naïve tone.

"First, dump the water out of them and put them on. Then you wear 'em 'til you go to bed. When you take them off don't set them too close to the fireplace. In the morning, put them on and wear them all day, even if they're wet. They will dry out in a few days and by then they'll fit your feet perfectly."

Wearing water-soaked boots was a rather distasteful experience, and when I took them off, I hid them from Aunt Mabel. That evening, I could not sleep because I was sure that my new boots were ruined, besides my feet felt weird. During the night, I went downstairs to check on them. They were still damp, so I went back to bed.

The next morning I had difficulty putting my boots on and I was worried that they had been ruined. I was surprised that by late afternoon they actually felt much better.

Cliff arrived about noon and began to tend to more cattle and calves. "How are the boots?" he shouted as I chased the member of the herd toward the Squeeze Pen.

"They're good," I said as I wiggled my toes.

"Good?" he asked as he turned to face me.

"Well better than good, I … I guess."

He leaned against his truck and pulled out his pipe. His eyes narrowed and I felt as if he were Principal Milligan at Connaught Elementary School.

"Yah, they're nice and feel pretty good," I said as I turned in a circle so he could see them. I wiggled my toes in the boots and then looked up at him. But before I could get out another word, he knelt down in front of me.

"OK," he said, "Let me ask you to do a favor for me."

"Me? OK. What do you want me to do?"

"Run," he said, "over to the windmill and run back."

When I returned he looked at me, "Well? What do you think?"

"Yah, they're not as stiff. They're good!"

"See, I told yah to trust me," he said as he puffed on his pipe.

That evening, I left my boots near the fireplace and after supper I carried them up to my room and placed them by my bed.

The next afternoon, Cliff returned with something in the back of his truck. It was not very large and yet it was fatter and larger than a calf. As I approached his truck, I could see that it was a small horse, and it had a saddle on it.

Cliff backed the truck up to a small embankment and then opened the tailgate. After stepping into the back of the truck, he pushed the small horse, and it backed out of the truck.

Unable to speak, I just stood there and watched.

"I need someone to ride this pinto and get him into shape. Do you think you can handle that?"

I nodded as I tried to close my mouth.

"By the way, his name is Donut. He has nice markings with the brown and white, and has long white sox," said Cliff as he tied the horse to a post.

"Why is he a … a pinto and what are socks?"

"A pinto is a brown and white horse, and if you look at

his legs, just above the hooves, he has long white legs. We call them socks."

Within a few moments, he showed me how to put my boot into the stirrup and climb into the saddle. "Here are the reins. If you want him to turn left, you lean the reins to the left and if you want to go to the right, just lean the reins to the right. It is called 'Neck Reining'. When you want him to stop, just pull back on the reins."

"Will he try to buck me off?"

"Not a champion rider like you. After all, you have your chaps, new boots and that hat. Where are your gloves?"

As I reached in my pocket for my gloves, Cliff continued. "By the way, I meant to ask you about that hat. It was white and now it looks kinda dirty."

"It got dirty at the rodeo."

He puffed on his pipe for a moment and smiled at me. "Yah, I remember."

I returned a smile, "What is Donut like?"

"He's a gentle horse," Cliff said as he slapped the butt of the horse.

"How do I make him go?" I ask, sounding eager to begin.

"Nudge him in the ribs with the heels of your boots and click your tongue."

I grabbed the saddle horn and nudged him and he started to walk.

"If you want him to go faster, nudge him harder," called Cliff as he struck a match to relight his pipe.

"How do I make him stop?" I asked, eager to learn.

"Pull back on the reins and say WHOA."

When I returned to where Cliff was standing, I asked, "Why is he short? Is he young?"

"He's quite young but is well behaved. Never did grow much from the day I bought him. I found him several years ago at an auction sale in Calgary."

"Who named him Donut?"

"I don't know what his name was before I bought him. I guess I gave him that name moments after I bought him 'cause I was chewing on a donut when I won the bid. The name stuck for all these years and he seems to know it."

For the next four days, I only left the saddle to eat lunch, go to the bathroom and to lead Donut out of the trees, where he often would go for the shade after our long afternoon rides.

Then on the fifth day, Aunt Mabel asked me to ride out to see if I could find the herd of cattle. The last thing I heard her say was, "And, be sure to count them. There aughta be thirty one of 'em."

For the next hour, I rode over hills, down trails and between tall trees until I spotted the herd near a small stream. As I approached, I began to count them and about the time I said 28, I noticed the black yearling standing nearby and he was pawing the ground again.

Donut seemed to know that not all was well and he started to turn from the herd. I tried to make him go forward but he was determined that it was time to leave. It was at that moment that the black yearling started to trot toward us.

"Donut!" I screamed and the race was on.

I may have had the reins in my hand but the saddle horn was all that mattered. Donut galloped as fast as his short legs would carry us. I tried to look over my shoulder, but my hat fell off and in my attempt to grab it, I lost hold of the saddle horn. The last thing I remembered seeing was the black yearling gaining on us just before I lost my balance and tumbled off, landing on the hard ground.

My head and shoulder hit the ground and all the air seemed to come out of me. I tried to move but nothing worked. Gasping for air, I tried to sit up and then I got nauseated. I had no idea how long I lay there but when I was able to breathe again, the first thing I thought about was the black yearling bull.

I wasn't sure when he had stopped running after us, but Donut was nowhere in sight. I finally got to my feet and started walking back to the ranch. It was a painful hour before I could see Aunt Mabel's buildings in the distance. As I was nearing the creek, I could hear the old Fargo truck coming toward me, so I sat down to clear my head. What was I to say to her when she arrived?

She stopped the truck and walked over to me. "Well, well Mr. Rodeo Man. What happened?" She looked at me before helping me to my feet. "Where's your hat?"

"Must be back by the herd. It fell off and that made me fall off Donut."

"The hat made you fall off!" she said as she helped me back to the truck.

"Next you'll tell me that the only reason that you're still alive is because of the chaps and boots." She sighed loudly, "Well, let's find that hat. By the way, how many were in the herd, or did you forget to count them?" She sounded a bit upset.

As we drove the pain in my side and shoulder almost took my breath away. Every bump made me gasp for air.

"There it is. Your hat's over there," she said. "And there's the herd."

"I … I counted them," I wheezed, "and there were thirty-one of 'em."

All the way home, Aunt Mabel said nothing. I was afraid that she was angry. When we arrived at the ranch, I could see Donut grazing by the barn.

"Who took off his saddle?" I asked meekly.

"The same person who was worried sick about you and the same person, who drove the Fargo to find you." After a few moments of silence, she leaned over and hugged me, and I moaned from the pain.

That evening, while we were sitting on the porch, she asked me why I fell off, and I told her how the black yearling had chased me, and then I told her about what happened at the Squeeze Pen.

Closing her eyes and shaking her head, she sighed, "I know that black yearling has a bad attitude, 'cause it comes from stock that was tough to handle. But I had no idea that he's that dangerous." She sipped the last few drops of tea and turned to me. "You could have died out there today, yah know?"

I felt like I had, but said nothing.

"Well, at least you would have died with your boots on," she said as she opened the screen door and went inside.

"Maybe it was the chaps and the boots that saved me," I whispered as I tried to take another uncomfortable breath.

Every time I closed my eyes to try to sleep that night, all I could see was the black yearling running toward me, my hat flying off and me falling off Donut. It was a sleepless and painful night. Finally, in the orange glow of the morning light, I fell into an exhausted sleep.

CHAPTER 6

AN AUNT I DIDN'T KNOW

B

ANG! BANG! BANG! BANG! BANG!

The sound and the echo were so distinct that I sat up in bed. It was the sound of a rifle, a big rifle. I had heard small rifles like a .22 and BB gun, but this was a big, powerful rifle. The BB gun that I had received for my birthday had a soft sound to it and the .22 rifle that my father used to shoot gophers did not compare to this rifle.

BANG! BANG! BANG! BANG! BANG!

I jumped from bed and called for my aunt but there was complete silence. Partially dressed, I ran down the stairs and stopped on the porch to pull on my pants and boots. The screen door slammed behind me as I zipped up my pants and held my breath.

BANG! BANG! BANG! BANG! BANG!

My ears were ringing even though there was silence. The echo had come from every building on the ranch and it made it difficult to tell where the gunshot came from. Anxious, I ran to the far end of the porch and looked toward the garden but there was no sign of my aunt. Running to the other end of the porch, I could see that the Fargo was still in the garage. Then I realized that Fritz was nowhere to be found. He must be with Aunt Mabel.

I called as loud as I could, but there was nothing but an echo of my voice among the buildings and hundreds of trees. I called a second time and then I thought I heard my aunt's voice calling from the barn.

Running toward the barn, I tried to button my shirt but running and buttoning didn't seem to work. After climbing over the fence, I rounded the corner of the barn. There in front of me lay the black yearling bull and it seemed to breathing its last. A deep gurgled moan came from its mouth as it tried to move its head but its eyes began to close. Blood dripped from his forehead and from his nose, making small streams of blood on his satin, curly hair.

Unsure of what had happened, I ran around to the rear of the barn. I peered around the corner to see my aunt lying on the ground, trying to crawl into the shade of the building. In her hands, she held a large rifle, the kind that we used to see on the television show, The Rifleman.

Her eyes met mine and she called in a soft whisper. "I'm … hurt son." She tried to take a breath. "You … need to … get me … to the doctor … as fast … as you can." She paused to take a short breath. "Get … the Fargo. The keys are in it."

Each word was punctuated with a slow gasp. She closed her eyes as she continued to grip the rifle. Beside her lay Fritz, who seemed unsure of what he should do next. He licked the back of her hand and placed his head on the ground next to her.

I took off my shirt to cover her and ran to get the truck. I had never driven it before, but I had watched her shift as she drove. Now I had to learn. I ran as fast as I could, stumbling as I rounded the corner of the house on my way to the garage.

As I put the clutch in with my left foot, I reached for the key and pushed the starter button. The engine growled and suddenly started. I wiggled the gear shift to find reverse to back the Fargo out of the garage. After three tries, the truck started to back out of the garage. Once outside, I searched for a forward gear and started for the barn. As I inched toward the barn, I decided to drive close to the barn but not so close that I had to use reverse again.

My aunt was very small but I was unable to lift her because every time I tried, she would cry out in pain, so I lay her back on the ground. Panic gripped me and fear overwhelmed me when I thought she could die. Blood dripped from the corner of her mouth, and I realized that she was still holding the rifle.

"Get the blanket ... behind the seat ... the seat of the truck ... and bring it," she whispered. She coughed several times and she suddenly became pale. I was sure she was dying.

As she gasped for air, I ran to the truck and returned with the blanket. She told me to lay on the ground next to her. Then she slowly and painfully rolled onto it and whispered, "This is up ... up to you son. Drag me ... to the truck." At no time did she lay the rifle down, but held it in both of her hands as if her life depended on it.

It seemed like forever but I finally had her next to the truck. She looked up at me with the most intense stare I have ever seen. "Give me … a moment to rest," she whispered. She closed her eyes, and I felt as if I had been punched in the stomach.

"You … have to get … me into the back … of the truck," she whispered as she coughed and then I saw blood trickling from her left nostril. Her life was now my responsibility.

"This … is going to hurt," she gasped. "I don't think … you can lift me … but …" She closed her eyes again. "There is no other way … son," She coughed several times, held her breath and then spit blood onto the ground next to my cowboy boots.

I stared in silence, not knowing what to do next. My heart pounded in my bony chest.

"Try to sit … sit me up." She paused as she tried to breathe and then continued, "and come … from behind me … and put your arms under my armpits," she wheezed and then gasped for air. A loud moan gurgled in her throat.

"Please … don't die," I whispered.

She tried to smile as she rolled slightly to one side. I leaned forward. "OK, when I …" again she coughed and her blood dripped onto my arm. "When I say now … you lift … with all your might."

"OK."

"Are you ready?" Her voice faded off into a whisper.

I nodded my head and said, "Uh-huh."

"OK, now." Her last word was lost in my loud groan as I lifted with all of my strength. Both of us wobbled from side to side but before I knew it she was standing. She leaned against the back of the Fargo and a moment later I grabbed both of her legs and pushed her bum into the back of the truck. She closed her eyes as she lay on her side. Blood now flowed in a steady stream from the corner of her mouth and from her nostril. She continued to cling to the rifle.

"Good, boy … you'd make a fine medic. Now go … to the house and bring … all the pillows … that you can find." She paused to catch her breath, "And several blankets. Hurry … son. Time … may be running out."

I ran to the house as fast as my boots would allow me to and let the screen door slam behind me. The first pillow that I grabbed was the one I used to sleep on. Then I ran through the house grabbing pillows, towels and two blankets.

When I returned she appeared grey and not breathing. For a moment I thought she was dead. "Aunt Mabel, please don't die," I whispered as I touched her arm.

"Put that … red pillow … by my ribs … and that one by my arm. Good." Again she coughed and more blood ran down her cheek. "Now roll up … the blanket and put it … on my abdomen. Good boy. You're doing well. Don't leave me, boy. It's now … that I need you the most."

Sweat was pouring from my brow and for a moment I wished that this were a dream, and I would wake up to find everything as it was before.

"The last pillow … that's it … put it under my head. Good. Let's go," she whispered. "I know the road … is rough but drive to Cliff's Ranch. Let's … go."

Before I started to drive, I placed a pillow under my seat so I could see out of the windshield. The ride to Cliff's ranch would be slow for I only knew how to get to third gear. When I looked down I could see that my pants were covered in blood.

I remembered nothing of the road or whether it was smooth or rough. All I remembered was the look in her eyes before I left her side. She was a small woman but strong and tougher than any guy that I had ever met.

When we were half way to Cliff's ranch, I stopped and ran to the back of the truck to see if Aunt Mabel was still alive. There she lay with the rifle by her side. The color on her face and lips reminded me of my uncle at his funeral. She was white and her lips were blue, except for the red blood on her cheek and jaw.

"Please, don't die, Aunt Mabel. Please," I pleaded as she touched my arm, coughed and moaned.

I got back into the truck, and kept trying to avoid the potholes. I must admit that some of the time I did not see the road for the tears in my eyes. I stopped a second time and ran back to see if she was still alive and all she did was try to smile.

When I stopped in front of the Cliff's house, I beeped the horn several times and Cliff stepped out of the barn and walked slowly toward the truck. He narrowed his brows as I jumped out of the truck.

"IT'S AUNT MABEL! SHE'S HURT REAL BAD! HURRY, CLIFF!"

"What the hell?" he said, as he ran toward us and when he arrived, he reached out to touch her. She did not move and I closed my eyes 'cause I did not want to see if she was dead.

"Cliff," she whispered. "I'm hurt … real bad. I … think my … my ribs are broken," she paused to cough and moaned loudly. "My insides … have been hurt … and I'm … coughing up blood. The black yearling … he … he …"

"You sit with her," said Cliff to me. "I'll drive. If things are too rough, tap on the rear window."

Soon we were racing down the road for town. I didn't look at the road because of tears. I knelt beside Aunt Mabel so that I could hold her hand. The ride was very cold because I had forgotten to put on a shirt so I wrapped one of the blankets around me.

"I've never seen anyone die before except on television. Please don't die, Aunt Mabel," I pleaded as tears ran down my hot cheeks. The edges of the blanket flapped against me as we raced down the dirt road. I closed my eyes and whispered, "Please God. We need your help. I mean Aunt Mabel needs your help. Don't let her die. Please. I don't know what else to say."

When I opened my eyes she smiled, and a moment later Cliff slowed for a sharp corner in the road. It seemed like eternity before we arrived in town. Cliff raced through town beeping the horn to warn people to get out of the way. I was glad he knew where he was going. Time seemed to be our worst enemy.

The hospital was small. Two nurses appeared after Cliff ran into the building. They placed Aunt Mabel onto a bed with wheels, took the rifle from her hands and then pushed the bed into the building. Soon she was out of sight.

I stood alone by the entrance of the hospital. No one came to talk to me, so I walked up the stairs into a waiting room. There were six single plastic covered chairs and one cloth couch, so I sat down. Time did not exist. There was no sound and no sense to all of this. I looked up at the clock on the wall and it was almost ten o'clock.

I ran my hand through my hair and I realized that I hadn't brushed it before coming to town. Looking at my hands, I could see blood and dirt, so I walked over to the men's bathroom to wash my hands and arms.

No one came to the waiting room, so I sat there and waited. By one o'clock, I had counted the squares of linoleum on the floor, the number of curtains, and the number of windows. Still no one came.

The thought struck me that maybe Aunt Mabel was dead. I knelt by one of the padded chairs, folded my hands and closed my eyes. "God, I have a very sick aunt in this hospital. I know that you know it too, but please don't let her die. Please." Tears rolled down my cheeks and I had to wipe them with the back of my hand 'cause I had no shirt to wipe them on.

"My Sunday School teacher, Mr. Janke, told us that you love people and take no pleasure in our pain and she has pain, if she is still alive. I've never really asked for a favor as serious as this one. I mean, you helped me pass into grade 6 this year, gave me a brother and things like that, but this favor is more serious. Don't let her die. Please." Not knowing what else to say, I ended my prayer with "Amen," and remained on my knees for a long time.

Later I decided to walk down the hallway to the double doors that led down the hall but stopped because I knew that nurses never let you go into a hospital unless you were thirteen years old. Eventually I walked back to the waiting room and lay on the couch.

Someone touched me and I sat up. It was a nurse and Cliff was with her.

"It's five o'clock. Have you had anything to eat?" the nurse asked.

"No!" I rubbed my eyes before blurting out, "I want to know how she is. Is she dead?" My voice cracked with fear and exhaustion.

"No, no. She's not dead. She'll be here for a few days but you're coming to my house until she comes home from the hospital," said Cliff.

"What happened?" I asked.

"I'll tell you on the way home. Come with me," Cliff said as he helped me to my feet.

"You must be cold. Here's a shirt," the nurse said as she handed me a small faded shirt and one of the blankets that we had used on our trip to the hospital. Then Cliff and I went out to the truck and started for home.

We drove for a long time in silence and when I could stand it no longer, I asked, "What happened to her?"

"She was in the corral checking a cow and the black yearling charged at her, and she barely got out of the way. She had to hide under the old hay wagon for awhile and when it was safe to escape, she climbed over the fence and went to the house for her rifle."

"Yeah, so how did she get hurt, and when did she shoot the yearling?"

"When she returned, he charged at her again so she fired a shot into the air to scare him but he didn't stop coming. He knocked her down and while she was lying on the ground, she shot him."

"But there were two bullet holes in him. Weren't there?" I interrupted.

"When he tried to get up again, she shot him a third time."

"Will she live? How did she learn to shoot like that?"

"You don't know your aunt, do you?"

"No," I said in a partial whisper as I wiped my nose with the back of my hand.

"She was a nurse in the army during the war in Europe. She saved the lives of soldiers while they lay on the battlefield. On several occasions, she had to use a rifle to keep the enemy from coming near. She and the other nurses were very valuable. They were quite a unit."

"Aunt Mabel was in the army?" I asked as my mouth dropped open.

"Yes and she was wounded and in a POW camp too, and survived."

"What is a POW camp?"

"POW stands for prisoner of war," he replied. "She and three others actually escaped. She's a marvelous lady but there's a tough streak in her a mile wide. Look at the pain she was in," said Cliff and he shifted gears to round a corner in the road.

"So why did she kill the black yearling?"

"You never knew your Uncle John, did you?"

"Uncle John who?"

"Big man about two hundred and eighty pounds. He met Mabel and together they bought the ranch. About a year ago, he was killed by a bull with a bad disposition."

"A bull … Uncle John … killed? I never heard about this."

"She heard your story about the black yearling charging you while you were riding Donut and when she went out today and he charged her. That did it. So she shot him."

Cliff slowed the truck and we turned into his yard. "Come in and have something to eat. You can bunk in one of my rooms. We'll see her tomorrow."

We ate but I don't remember what Cliff put on my plate. After he cleaned up the table, he pointed to a doorway, "In that room is a bunk. When you're ready, help yourself."

I stepped out into the night air to have a pee before going to bed. The clear sky was so beautiful and the stars were so bright against that dark sky. A quarter moon seemed to own the eastern sky. After some time, I opened the door to Cliff's house, walked down the dim hallway and felt around in the darkness for a bed. All I could think about was Aunt Mabel, the war, the black yearling and an Uncle John whom I had never met.

As I lay on the bed, I wondered if mom and dad knew Uncle

John. How come we never heard about this? Was there more I didn't know about?

As I pulled the covers to my chin, the thought occurred to me, that Aunt Mabel was an aunt that I didn't really know.

CHAPTER 7

FRITZ, THE HERO

Bright light awakened me. I sat up and blinked my eyes several times when Cliff opened the curtains to my room. If I had seen what was on the walls in the bedroom before I went to sleep, I wouldn't have slept at all.

"Time to do some work, Young'un. So let's eat. See you in the kitchen," Cliff said as he walked through the doorway and disappeared down the hallway.

On the walls were heads of wild animals. On either side of the window were deer heads with antlers. To my left, was the head of a large black bear and in the corner next to the door was the head of a wolf. I looked to my right and saw a moose head and above the headboard of my bed was an elk. All of them seemed to be looking at me as if they were asking if I were the one that put them there. Dressing slowly, without taking my eyes off of them, I ran out of the room.

"Have a seat. Breakfast is ready," Cliff said as he pointed to my plate.

I looked at the meat for a moment, "None of this is from

the animals in my room, is it?" I asked as I finished buttoning my shirt.

"Nope. This is beef and eggs. It'll give you strength for the day. We have some unpleasant work to do at Mabel's ranch, so eat up."

I poked at it and tasted the meat. It was very good so I ate everything on my plate. When I was finished, Cliff pointed to the sink. "Go and wash the dishes and put them in the cupboard. Don't like leaving a messy kitchen," he said as he walked out of the house.

Washing dishes is not a job that I like, but in this case, he had cooked so I guessed that it was up to me to clean them. Smoke from his pipe came through the screen door as I washed and dried the dishes.

A half hour later, he entered the kitchen just as I was drying the last cup.

"Are you ready?" he asked.

"Yup, I'll be right there," and a few moments later I ran to his truck.

"What are we going to do?" I asked as we drove to Aunt Mabel's ranch.

He smiled, "You'll see," was all he said. The rest of the way to her ranch, I tried to think of what needed doing. When we arrived, he stopped in front of the house and we stepped from the vehicle. "Have you ever started or driven Mabel's tractor?" he asked as he slammed the door of his Ford.

"You mean that Cockshutt 40?"

"It's the only tractor she's got," he said briskly as he started for the tool shed.

I ran to the tractor and climbed into the seat and pushed the gearshift into neutral, turned the key and pressed the starter button. It turned over several times and when I pulled the choke lever it started. After adjusting the speed of the motor, I looked over at the tool shed to Cliff who was waving at me to drive over to where he was.

I pressed as hard as I could on the clutch and pulled it into gear. Unable to control the heavy clutch with my foot, it lurched forward and I grabbed the steering wheel so that I wouldn't fall off. When I arrived where Cliff was standing, I pressed the clutch and pushed the gear lever into neutral.

"I forgot about the heavy clutch on this type of tractor," said Cliff as he lifted several chains onto the hitch. "Once I've loaded these chains, I'll drive it."

In a moment, he climbed up and sat on the seat as I clung to the small curved fender.

He drove to the main gate of the corral and let me off so that I could open the gate. Once the gate was open, I climbed back onto the tractor and asked, "What are we going to do?"

"We need to pull the dead yearling out of the yard so coyotes or bears don't come by and disturb the chickens and other animals. 'Sides the other cattle don't like the smell of death," he continued as he drove the red Cockshutt tractor to where the dead bull lay.

"Looks like the herd has left," he said and then walked to the head of the yearling and knelt on one knee. He tipped his hat back and started to chuckle. "Mabel sure is a good shot. She told me that she fired a warning shot but the yearling kept coming. She must have fired the Winchester as she was trying to get out of the way. Wow! What a shot. She shot him right between the eyes as he was coming for her. I wonder if there's anything this woman can't do."

"But he has two holes in his forehead," I said as I stood

behind him to look at the bloody forehead of the dead beast. I must admit that even though I knew he was dead, I was shaking inside with the fear that he would suddenly stand to his feet.

"She shot him a second time as she lay on the ground. I guess she wanted to be sure that the bastar … I mean, beast didn't get up again."

"I found her around the corner, so why . . ?"

"She must have crawled away from him."

Then I noticed something moving by the side of the barn. It was Fritz. He wagged his tail but he didn't stand or come to me. "It's FRITZ!" I shouted as I ran to his side. He was severely bruised on the side of his head and shoulder. His body seemed uneven in size, larger on one side than the other side.

"DON'T TOUCH HIM!" yelled Cliff. "Use gloves. Even a friendly dog may snap at you when you touch 'em, especially if they're severely hurt. They don't mean any harm but they're simply reacting to pain."

Cliff knelt beside Fritz and gently brushed his head as he moaned and licked Cliff's glove. "Fritz must have been kicked by the yearling. He's been here all day and all night," Cliff said. "Dogs can be stoic and are able to endure pain, but being here this long may have made things worse."

I watched as Fritz licked Cliff's glove, "What do we do? Will he live?"

"I'll stay with him. You go and get a small container of water. He needs a bit of a drink. He's been here for a long time."

I ran as fast as I could. The tears in my eyes made it difficult to see the windmill water pump. I grabbed the bucket by the pump and pumped as hard and fast as I could. When it was partially full of water, I ran to Fritz's side. Much of the water splashed over the brim as I ran and wet my pants.

Fritz drank for a few moments and looked up at me. One of his eyes was badly bruised and seemed blurred. When he closed his eyes, he shook momentarily but when he tried to open them I saw that he couldn't open the injured eye.

"Will he be alright?" I asked hoping for only one answer.

"You stay with him while I drag this yearling out into the bush. I'll be back in half an hour. Don't let him drink any more. Just stay with him and comfort him," said Cliff as he removed his jacket and covered Fritz.

I watched as Cliff wrapped the chains around the hind legs of the black yearling and dragged it over the hill with the tractor. I could hear the sound of the tractor as it disappeared over the hill on its way to a grove of trees near some swampy land.

Fritz and I remained at the side of the barn. All I did was stay with him and brush his right paw. At one point, he tried to stand, but lost his balance and fell down into the position that we had found him in.

Off in the distance, I could hear the Cockshutt tractor. It was coming back to the barnyard. As Cliff drove past us, he shouted, "Stay here. I'll be back with the truck. We'll take Fritz to town to see the vet."

Cliff returned and we loaded Fritz into the front seat of the truck. He was obviously in pain, for his upper lip quivered as if he were going to bite us.

"Do you think he'll live?" I asked as I tried to swallow the lump in my throat.

Cliff said nothing all the way into town. The silence left me with a sad feeling, one that makes you nauseated. We finally arrived in town and stopped by a veterinarian, named Dr. Corbett. Cliff carried Fritz into the office, while I waited outside.

The wait was just like it was with Aunt Mabel at the hospital.

I walked around the truck several times and then sat on the running board. Cliff returned twenty minutes later and put his arm around me, "Well, we'd better go and see Mabel. What do you think about that?"

"What about Fritz?" I whispered, hoping that all would be alright.

"Corbett will take care of him. Fritz will be alright, just like Mabel. Both of them are tougher that you think."

When we arrived at the hospital, Cliff walked with me past the front desk and down the hall. When we passed the nurse's desk, a nurse looked at me and asked if I was thirteen.

Before I could say 'No', Cliff responded with, "He's just short of thirteen by a week or two and just a little short for his age too. Sides thirteen doesn't make you stronger and able to resist diseases; 'sides he's with me."

All she said was, "Oh, OK."

Cliff pushed the door to my aunt's room and called, "Maaaybelll. Are you there? It's us."

After a pause, I heard her voice and we went into her room. She was sitting on a large padded chair. Her face and arm were bruised and she had a large piece of cloth wrapped around her ribs.

"You're quite the boy," she said as she smiled at me. "If it weren't for you, I'd have died beside that barn. You're a real soldier." She paused to get her breath and said, "I'm proud of you, son," as several tears appeared in her eyes.

I wanted to say something but nothing came out of my mouth, so I swallowed and smiled.

She looked up at Cliff. "Fritz was injured by the yearling and I hope he's alright. I couldn't sleep last night when I remembered he was in the corral with me. Did you find him? Is he alright?"

"We just brought Fritz to the vet. He was by the barn alright," said Cliff as he pulled a chair to be next to Aunt Mabel to reach for her hand.

"He's hurt too but we're sure he'll live," I blurted out before she could say or ask anything else.

"Fritz! Poor Fritz. In all of the excitement, I remember him being kicked by the yearling and yelping as he fell to the ground. In my pain I forgot him," she said in an apologetic tone. "How could I have forgotten Fritz? He distracted the bull long enough for me to lever another bullet into the chamber of the rifle. He saved my life." She dabbed her eyes with a paper napkin.

Cliff patted her hand. "Fritz is with the Doc. Corbett. He'll be OK but what about you?"

"Well, I have three cracked ribs and I'm a bit sore in my stomach and pelvis. I guess that means that I'll have to rest on the porch while my hired man does the cooking and all the summer chores."

"Mabel, you know that both of us will do most anything for you," Cliff assured her as he winked at me. He reached and brushed a stray curl from her forehead.

She smiled and raised her other hand to me so I stepped closer and held it. It was the first time that I felt an urgency to let her know that I really liked her, so I squeezed her hand.

"I'd hug both of you but I'm too sore," she wheezed and then tried to chuckle.

"Please get well," I whispered. "I ... I prayed for you. I hope you don't mind."

You and Fritz and, of course Cliff are my best ..." she suddenly held her ribs and tried to resist a cough.

"I thought you were going to die, so I ..." I was unable to finish my sentence for my tongue seemed unable to move.

She squeezed my hand and then insisted that we check on Fritz before we leave town. We remained with her; me holding her hand with a large bruise on it and Cliff, well, he removed his hat and pulled out his pipe.

"Cliff you can't smoke in here. This is a hospital."

"Hospitals always have rules, don't they?"

Cliff and I drove over to Corbett's Veterinary Clinic to see Fritz. As Cliff and I walked into the office, the lady at the front counter turned to call Dr. Corbett.

"Fritz will have to stay a little longer. He's had the stuffin' knocked out of him. Right now, he's resting after some surgery and wouldn't be able to go home anyway. Maybe in a couple of days," Corbett said. "His most serious injury is his eye. I'm afraid he will lose sight in it … maybe even lose the eye completely."

I wanted to say something but Cliff put his hand on my shoulder and squeezed lightly. "OK, Doc. We'll see yah then," Cliff said and turned me toward the door.

Before we left town, Cliff stopped at the grocery store and when he returned he handed me an ice cream cone. Boy did that taste good and somehow the world seemed better. Aunt Mabel and Fritz would be home in a few days.

At about five thirty, we started for home and somewhere between Ghost River and Pine Falls, I fell asleep.

CHAPTER 8

THE CHURCH DIVING BOARD

Fritz was allowed to come home two days later. He had two teeth missing and his right eye had been severely injured. Dr. Corbett said he could see very little with it. Fritz never left my side and I noticed that he was rather reluctant to go near the barn and corral from that time on. The incident with the black yearling must have stolen his courage.

Aunt Mabel stayed in the hospital for about a week before the doctor would let her go home. From then on, Aunt Mabel and Fritz were closer than ever. They spent the next week on the porch, while Cliff and I were busy painting, fixing fence, cooking and washing dishes. In fact, Fritz gained status with Aunt Mabel because she allowed him to sleep in the house after the terrible incident.

Most evenings, I went to bed without eating because I was too tired for supper. Breakfast was my time to eat. Three eggs, sausages, fried potatoes and six slices of toast, all capped off with three glasses of milk and two cookies. I even tried to drink coffee, but decided that I would leave that to Cliff and Aunt Mabel.

"A growing boy needs to eat," Cliff said as he poured himself another cup of coffee. He and Aunt Mabel always drank their coffee on the porch, while I ate at the kitchen table.

I stepped out onto the porch as Aunt Mabel set her cup on the handrail. "Tomorrow is Sunday." she said as she adjusted her apron, "You need to take a day off. How would you like to go to a summer camp by Gull Lake?"

"A camp? What kind of camp?" I asked as I swallowed the last piece of toast I was chewing on.

"It's a church camp. You've been here for several weeks and we haven't been to church and I know that your family goes to church, so let's go. Oh, and be sure to bring your swimming suit with you."

"Swimming suit? Why do I need a swimming suit at church?"

"It's next to a big lake and many kids usually swim after church. 'Sides, you could probably use some fun about now. We've worked you pretty hard. There will be many young men and women your age, so let's go and have a good time."

"Do they have Sunday School there?" I asked, unsure of what a church camp was like.

She smiled as she sipped on the last few drops of coffee in her cup.

"What about Cliff? Will he be coming too?" I asked as I looked at him.

Cliff raised his cup to me. "Church is for good people like you and Mabel. I'm too old and crusty. You go with Mabel and have fun."

Sunday morning arrived and after breakfast, Aunt Mabel

and I drove to Gull Lake. She did not drive very fast because of the bumpy roads. Every time she shifted gears, she seemed to sigh and I could tell that she was still in some pain.

After turning off the main road, we drove down a dirt road that was totally shadowed by large fir and poplar trees. It wove around many trees and several sloughs but it was smooth because it seemed to be made of pure sand. We stopped next to about fifty cars and trucks and started to walk toward a large building in the distance. I could hear the people singing a hymn that sounded like, 'How Great Thou Art.' The piano seemed sadly out of tune or the player did not know how to play very well.

It was a bright sunny day, so we stopped at the entrance to the large building for a moment to let our eyes adjust to the darkness in the building. We stepped into the building where the people were sitting and sat in the back row with the ushers. I had never been allowed to sit in the back row before, so this was a new experience for me. The church I attended, with my parents, was different because the men sat on one side, the women on the other side and young people like me sat in the front pews. Here everyone sat wherever they wanted to. This was neat. I already liked this church and had only been here for a few minutes.

In the church that my family attended there seemed to be an unspoken set of rules. When you were a young child, you had to sit with your mother and when you were eight or twelve, you sat in the front rows, but when you were thirteen or older, you sat with your father. Soon, I would be able to sit with my father and the older men.

Three guitars, one accordion, a bass fiddle and an old upright piano were playing as the congregation sang loudly. I noticed that Aunt Mabel was trying to sing too but she seemed unsure of the words. I suspected that her ribs also hurt because she smiled at me and sat down to hold her side. When I looked over at her, she was reading the words as the congregation sang.

A trio of ladies started to sing and when they started the second verse, someone nudged my leg. I looked up and there was Cliff. He just stood there with his hat in his hand and looked at me. Instantly, I moved over to make room for him. Aunt Mabel smiled at him. I was so excited to see him that I almost said his name out loud.

Just as a man stood up to start the sermon, I felt as if someone was looking at me. My eyes met those of a dark haired girl who was wearing a red dress. She was about my age and was sitting three rows ahead of us. She smiled and turned away so her long black curls covered her face.

Momentarily stunned, I tried to remember if I had ever seen her before. She looked over her shoulder and smiled again, but I was afraid to move, after all, I was in church. I was sure the she didn't know me and I didn't know her. When she looked away, I turned around to see if she was looking at someone behind me, but to my embarrassment, there was only an unpainted wooden wall.

The sermon was about Adam and Eve and how Satan used a snake to tempt Eve into disobeying God. After Eve had tasted the fruit, she gave it to Adam and he ate some too. All of this got him into a lot of trouble.

Cliff leaned over and whispered into my ear. "Women: if you obey them you find yourself in trouble, even if God is somewhere nearby."

I knew that Aunt Mabel heard him because she closed her eyes and shook her head from side to side.

For the next half-hour the man enthusiastically preached

his sermon and I could tell that Cliff was a bit restless, for he often winked at me and then looked towards Aunt Mabel. She would look at him out of the corner of her eye and he would take a large breath and straightened his posture.

While I was trying to guess how this part of the sermon would help me in everyday life, I noticed that the girl looked back at me again. From where I was sitting, she appeared to have blue eyes. Her thick black hair, along with her red dress, made it hard for me to concentrate on the sermon. I looked up at Cliff, who smiled, shook his head from side to side and then raised his eyebrows and winked. "I bet her name is Eve. Trust me I've seen this all before."

She was the prettiest girl I had ever seen. I tried to guess what her name might be. Maybe it was Rosella, Veronica or even Marilyn. I looked at her again and then up at Cliff. This time he shrugged his shoulders and tried to frown but his raised eyebrows let me that he knew what boys think about.

Maybe her name was Georgina, Julie, Jane or ... maybe Cliff was right. Her name was probably Eve. EVE? That is what the minister was talking about.

I picked up a tattered songbook and paged through it to keep from looking at her. Sometime later everyone stood and after closing prayer, we were allowed to leave the building. Many people came over to speak with Aunt Mabel and they seemed pleased that Cliff had taken the time to come to church too. Both of them were more popular than I had imagined.

After the service everyone seemed to make their way down to the dining hall. The adults seemed more interested in conversation than dinner. Cliff and I felt a little uncomfortable about being there.

When a man behind us asked Cliff if he was the man that

won the Bull Riding Buckle three years in a row at the Sundre rodeo in the town of Sundre, I was shocked for I had no idea that Cliff was a bullrider. They seemed to have something in common and started talking about many other things. Cliff discovered that the other man had been in a bull riding event in the Ponoka Stampede. Their conversation seemed to make their wait less boring.

I, on the other hand, was bored so I started to look around to see if I could spot that dark haired girl with the red dress. She was nowhere to be seen. The line of people moved very slowly and after about half an hour, Aunt Mabel, Cliff and I stepped into the dining hall. The food smelled so good that my stomach growled several times. My aunt nudged me and both of us began to laugh. As we laughed, I realized that I liked her more than I had imagined.

With my plate filled high with food, I moved down the narrow aisles and looked for a place to sit. Several times, I almost dumped my plate because someone stood up without looking. When I sat down, my aunt leaned over to me, "I was looking for the young girl with the red dress. It would be nice to talk to her, don't you think? She seems to like you."

"Nah," I said as I took a large mouthful of mashed potatoes and gravy.

Two boys who were sitting across from me and one of them said, "Hi" but I just nodded and continued to eat.

"My name is Dale," said the older one. "And this is Craig. We're from the town of Olds. Where are you from?"

"I'm from the city but I'm living on my aunt's ranch for the summer. Maybe you've heard of it. It's called the Broken Antler Ranch."

"No, I haven't heard of it," responded Dale.

Our conversation continued, while we emptied our plates and three desserts. They seemed to be nice guys so I walked outside with them.

"Have you ever been here before?" Dale asked.

"Nah," I said as I pulled up my pants and spit on the ground.

"Well, let us show you around. You'll like this place. First, we'll show you the rope tower, then the corrals, the meadow and finally the swimming area down by the lake. Come on let's go."

An hour later, we arrived on the beach of a very clear lake. It was easy to see the sand and rocks at the bottom. Some distance from shore, there was a diving board that floated on large metal barrels. Around all of this area was a floating fence with orange floating plastic jugs so boaters would not enter and injure the swimmers. There must have been a hundred kids in the lake. Occasionally, the lifeguard blew a whistle but generally these kids were having the time of their lives.

"Did you bring a swim suit?" asked Dale.

"Yup, but it's in the truck,"

"We'll get our swimming suits and see you in that changing hut," said Craig as both of them ran through the trees toward their vehicle. I started for the Fargo. When I returned with my swimsuit, I went into the changing hut but did not see them. After changing into my swim suit, I stepped outside and walked along the sandy beach for five minutes until I spotted them in the water. The bottom of the lake was sandy and the water was cold as I waded into the lake. There was so much room; far more room than in the swimming pool on Bell Street.

Craig and I watched as Dale climbed the ladder of the diving board. Confidently, he walked to the edge, waved at us and then jumped off. It looked like fun but the diving board I was used to in the city swimming pool was not as high. Besides, I was not a diver and didn't swim very well.

I heard a girl's voice beside me so I turned and there, to my amazement was the dark haired girl that had waved at me in church.

"Hi. My name ith Alva. I thaw you in tchurth. Are you new here? Whath's your name?"

I swallowed and looked at Craig and back at her. "My name? Yes, I have been in church before. 'Sides I … don't come here … very often," that is all I managed to say as my voice cracked and I felt my cheeks get warm. She looked different with her wet hair, and she appeared older than Craig or me.

"Hi Craig," she said as she turned and ran into the water. Moments later she bobbed, her head above the surface.

I was unsure of what happened. It sounded as if she had a lisp and I couldn't believe that a girl so nice looking could have … a lisp.

Again she called to Craig and me, "Hurry cauth the water isth nicth."

"Hi, Alva," Craig managed to whisper.

Just then Dale waved to us and jumped off the board again. He made a large splash and Alva raised her arm and cheered. "Yessth."

Craig and I waded into the water as Alva asked, "Do you ever thjump or dive?" Her girlish voice made my mouth feel dry.

"In the city pool, I always dive but here … I need … need time to look it over first."

"Come withh me and I'll thow you how to do it." As she spoke, a large motorboat roared past out of the fenced off area and I was not sure what else she said. I tried to look as if I understood.

"Thith will be eethzy for thomeone aths big ath you," she said. How could my throat feel so dry with all this water around me? At that moment, I knew what Adam felt like when he was in the garden and Eve asked him to bite into the apple. How she could ask me to jump off a high board like that one, made no sense to me but what made even less sense was that I considered doing it?

Just then Dale surfaced in front of us. "Come on, Alva and I will show you how much fun this can be," and with that both of them started swimming for the diving board.

"The water's too cold to be diving, after all we just ate and we might get cramps," I said to Craig as we floated in the water. He smiled and both of us watched as Alva and Dale climbed to the top of the diving board and recklessly jumped off. They seemed so free.

"I'm afraid too," whispered Craig in a defeated tone.

I ignored his comment but deep inside I was not sure if I could ever jump off something that high. After he smiled at me I added, "That board must be at least one hundred feet off the water."

"My dad helped build it," said Craig. "He said it was twelve feet high."

Again I ignored his comments but a moment later Alva and Dale appeared in front of us.

"Come on. This is fun," encouraged Dale.

Alva smiled at me, "You're not afraid, are you? Thomeone asth big and sthrong aths you? Thurely you're not afraid." She blinked her blue eyes and I willingly sank below the surface.

When I came up for air, she grabbed my arm. "Come on" she said.

"OK, I'll come," I said but all the way to the diving board

and up the stairs, I wondered why I felt the need to kill myself for someone with a lisp and a funny name like Alva.

Dale and Alva waited at the top of the diving board, while I climbed to my death. As I climbed I remember hearing that a gallows always has thirteen steps but this one … had more. When I reached the top of the diving board, I hung onto the handrail with all my might. This was higher than I imagined and was certainly much higher than the diving board at the pool on Bell Street.

"Do you want to go first?" asked Dale as his open hand pointed the way.

"Ladies first," I managed to say, even though my confidence was miles from this lake. I wanted to tell them about my winning ride at the rodeo and all the other things I had accomplished over my last few years of my life, but I couldn't trust my voice. Certain words sounded good but others cracked and some were only whispers.

Dale stepped to the front of the board, waved and disappeared. After the loud splash, he appeared and shouted, "Hurry! The water is great."

Alva stepped to the edge of the board and disappeared. After a loud splash, she came to the surface. "Iths great and lotha fun. Come on. Don't be thuch a thicken."

The diving board was on a floating raft and as the breeze blew and the motorboats roared past, the diving board swayed back and forth. Suddenly, I felt nauseated. I was unsure which would be worse, throwing up this high off the ground or killing myself when I hit the water?

In a moment, two younger boys pushed their way past me and jumped together. Instantly, the lifeguard blew the whistle. "ONE JUMPING AT A TIME! PLEASE!"

I walked to the edge of the board but the longer I stood there, the higher the board seemed to get. Riding calves was easier than jumping from up here. If I knew that the lifeguard was a doctor I might try this, but any courage that I once had, left me.

From below, I could hear Alva calling. "I thhink you're a thicken cawth you won't thump. THICKEN, THICKEN, THICKEN." Her voice fluctuated as she began to sing, "Nannanana."

Again two young boys passed me on their way to the end of the board. In an instant, they disappeared. How could they do this? Maybe farm kids were tougher than city kids.

The tower swayed from side to side and the longer I looked down at the surface of the water, the worse I felt.

Again, Alva called. "I THHINK YOU'RE A THICKEN."

I looked down at the ladder and since there was no one in my way, I started to climb down the ladder. This was not for me. Once I was back in the water, Dale came over to me and said, "I'll go with you if you want. I was afraid the first time I went, but now it's easy."

Alva appeared out of nowhere. "I thhink you're a thicken. I don't like thickens and you're a thicken or you'd thump."

For a moment, I wanted to forget that this was a church camp and drown her in front of everyone. I now knew how Adam felt. He was in trouble with no way out and I remembered that he did not get violent, so I considered other options.

Angry, I climbed up the ladder one more time and decided that if I was going to die, this was as good place as any. After all, I was at a church camp, I had attended church that morning and could show all of them what city folk are made of.

My toes gripped the edge of the board. I tried to lift one leg but it seemed as if it was glued to the board. I looked down at Craig and he waved. If I did this, it was for Craig and NOT for Alva or Dale.

I grabbed the tip of my nose and leaned forward. All sounds ceased. There were no kids below, no motorboats and no lifeguard whistles. My eyes were closed and I had no knowledge when the surface would kill me. My heart was pounding when I left the board but I was sure that it would stop as soon as feet felt air blowing between my toes.

I felt my forehead, neck and chest smack the water at the same time. It was like the time I rode my bicycle into the back of a parked car. I folded over, moved slowly to the surface and then tried to breath. Nothing worked. I gasped, but all I could do was; "Auggggggghhhhh." This was worse than my ride at the rodeo.

The sun seemed dim and I felt someone grab me by the arm and pull me. When I opened my eyes, I saw the lifeguard leaning over me. She was pushing on my chest and then I felt air going into my lungs. The warm sand on my back felt good but that was all that felt good.

"That was quite a splash," Dale said. "Better than any I've ever seen. I didn't know that you were that good. Can you do that again?"

"Auggggggggggggg."

"That wasth great."

I breathed as deeply as I could and tried to smile but my mouth was full of sand.

"Thaay, that wath the besth sthplasth I've ever theen," said Alva. "You're not a thicken! I'm sssorry for sthaying that."

I heard Cliff's voice. "Say, that was quite a splash. I didn't know that you liked swimming that much." After a moment of silence, I heard him again, "Can you see me?"

"Auggggggg."

I heard Aunt Mabel's voice but I couldn't understand a word. Her voice faded as I exhaled. When I inhaled I heard her say, "My God, son if you're going to die, you certainly picked a good place to do it." She sounded a little upset.

"Auggggggg."

"The boy's a damn fool," said Cliff as he lit his pipe and when smoke curled from his nostril he finished with, "and tough as a nail. But a damn fool."

"Cliffff," said Aunt Mabel. "This is a church and your language …"

"Auggggggggggg," was all that came out of my mouth.

Time passed and then I heard Cliff say, "Mabel we need to go 'cause its getting late. He'll be alright."

I remember her asking, "Are you sure?"

"When he's silent then we can worry but that aaaahhhhggga sound means he'll be OK."

I turned my head to see both of them walking toward the trees where the Fargo was parked. "We'll see you back at the truck in about ten minutes," said Cliff.

Didn't they know that I was one breath away from death? I sat up and wiped sand from my ears and mouth. After some encouragement from the lifeguard, I stood to my feet and staggered off to the changing hut. Before disappearing into the trees, I turned to wave at Dale and Craig but they were nowhere to be seen. The only one that waved at me was Alva.

I tried to button my shirt as I stumbled toward the Fargo and finally my lungs started to work again. I felt like I was about to lose all my dinner but then I managed to belch loudly and somehow that made me feel better. Better than what, I was not sure.

Cliff got into his truck and started to leave so we followed him down the winding road. I remembered what the minister said about Adam. "He willingly did something stupid for Eve because he liked her."

I wondered if Eve had dark hair, wore a red dress and had a lisp. Strange, but ultimately Adam died for his decision to listen to Eve and so could have I. It was amazing to me what I was willing to do for a girl I didn't know and I wasn't even in the Garden of Eden. What made this worse was that I was willing to do it for a girl that talked funny.

I remember Aunt Mabel turning the truck onto the main road. That is when I lay over on the seat because I was dizzy and fortunately fell asleep.

CHAPTER 9

POOR FOOTING IN CENTRE FIELD

Aunt Mabel must have been feeling better for she was very busy making pies and other desserts. Then one day, she told me that we were going to a community picnic at Keller's farm. A visit to Keller's farm seemed like a nice idea, besides Cliff and I did not have to fix the corral. I had never met the Keller's and when I asked how many people would be there, she smiled, wrinkled up her brow and said, "Suppose fifty or sixty. What do you think, Cliff?"

Cliff set his cup on the handrail on the porch and lit his pipe. "Last year there were about sixty three, I think."

"Will there be any kids my age?"

"Oh, yes, and there will be a ballgame, lots of sandwiches, an underground beef roast and lots of dessert. We've got to go. You'll love it."

"Wow! All of that on someone's farm?" I asked.

"Well, it's on their land but not on their farm. There is a

wonderful stand of trees, a small slough of water and an old ball diamond on their land, quite close to their farm buildings. There has been a picnic at that old ball diamond every summer for longer than anyone can remember."

As we loaded the Fargo, Aunt Mabel looked down at my cowboy boots. "Better bring your runners. Yah can't play ball with those boots and by the way, bring that ball glove of yours. It will likely be the only time that you get a chance to use it."

We followed Cliff to his ranch and then he drove the Fargo, while Aunt Mabel sat beside him. I felt a bit uncomfortable when she grabbed his arm and put her head on his shoulder, so I looked out the right side window.

We rode for about twenty-five minutes before turning north. The ride took us on several winding roads, past a small slough and over a very large hill. It was a sunny day and I was pleased that we were able to do something else, other than work. Besides swimming at a church camp was not my favorite memory because my chest still felt weird when I thought about Alva.

Cliff slowed the truck and we turned down a very rough road, with potholes, high weeds and overhanging tree branches that scratched the cab of the truck. We eventually entered a clearing and I was amazed at the number of trucks and people that were there.

Dozens of men were standing near some rough sawn seats behind a baseball diamond backstop. Some of the seats were broken and the backstop looked as if it would collapse the moment the first ball hit it. Off to my right, dozens of children were playing tag and several young girls were playing with skipping ropes. Nearby, smoke was coming out of a crooked chimney above a broken down shed. I was amazed at the number of tables in the clearing, all of which were covered with colorful table clothes.

Some distance from the old wooden building, I could see smoke coming out of the ground so I asked Cliff about it.

"That's an underground fire pit. The Keller's start by digging a rather deep hole and then, they place lotza split wood at the bottom of the hole and start the wood on fire. Once the fire is burning, they cover it in lots of coal and then some more wood. Eventually all that is in the hole is red hot coals, then they put large metal over the coals and place pieces of beef roast on it. Next they cover the meat with another large piece of metal so that it will roast. Then they cover it with a wet tarp and on top of that they place wet logs. The meat has been prepared 12 hours before it is put into the pit. Water needs to be splashed on the tarps so it won't burn but the water turns into steam and rises away from the meat. It cooks slowly. Wait until you taste it. It is fantastic."

Aunt Mabel nodded her head up and down. "You'll be surprise how tasty it is."

"What do they do to prepare the meat?"

"Well Keller, soaks the meat in a brine made of pickling spices, ketchup and brown sugar and leaves it on the meat for about 9 hours. Then he puts about 5 bottles of beer in the pot with the meat and it is ready in another 3 hours."

"Beer ... on meat?"

"Well Mr. Keller never did tell us his recipe so" she looked at Cliff before continuing, "he may use other spices and ..."

"Well," interrupted Cliff, "he may use some of his homebrew whiskey. Only he knows and he is not about to tell us and we, well we don't want to know. But it's good, just wait until you taste it. My mouth waters when I just think of it."

A little way down the road, I could see unpainted buildings: a house, a barn and three sheds. All of them seemed old and uncared for, not like the buildings on Aunt Mabel's Broken Antler Ranch. At least hers looked better now that Cliff and I had painted the fence and the buildings.

"This," Aunt Mabel said as Cliff shut off the motor, "is an annual picnic. It started so many years ago that those who started it are dead and their children's children just keep it going. I wouldn't miss it for anything. Someone said it started long before the war."

I looked at Cliff and he just smiled, opened the door and stepped out of the truck. Both of us carried Aunt Mabel's contribution of food to the broken down shed. Once inside, it was difficult to leave for every woman in the place wanted to meet me and some even touched my shoulder, others hugged me and one very large lady with large … ah well she ruffled my hair. Once free of the women, I raced to look for Cliff.

Cliff waved at me and so I walked over to where he and all of the men were standing. Some were chewing tobacco, others were smoking roll-your-own cigarettes and Cliff and two other men were smoking pipes. I made up my mind that when I was old enough to smoke, I would smoke a pipe, regardless of whether it stunted my growth or not.

Eventually I became bored, so I walked down to the small pond of water but found that cows had been in this water and left manure everywhere. There were hundreds of mosquitoes and other bugs, so I decided to leave.

Several bicycles passed me on the way to the ball diamond and several boys seemed to be fighting, so I returned to the truck. When I arrived, I sat in the shade of the truck and thought about the many things that I had done on Aunt Mabel's ranch. Wow, what a summer.

Off in the distance, I could hear a dinner bell ringing. Well, it was not actually a bell but a metal triangle, and I could see that the person ringing it wore a large apron. I started for the fragile old building and the closer I got, the hungrier I became.

I don't remember seeing so much food in one place. There were six kinds of salads, mashed and baked potatoes, gravy, vegetables and lots of soda pop.

Three men uncovered the underground roast pit and removed the meat from red-hot coals. I never knew that it was possible to roast small pig and large chunks of beef underground.

After my plate had been filled and emptied three times, I discovered that the dessert table was under a large tree. Six kinds of pies and five kinds of cake. This was an ideal place for a growing boy, I mean cowboy like me.

Cliff motioned for me to follow him and when we arrived at the pie table, we counted twenty three pies. This was the most wonderful picnic, ever.

After we had eaten, several of the men wandered over to the shade of a row of trees. Many of them lay in the grass and started to snore. It looked rather funny, twenty three men with full stomachs, snoring loudly enough to wake the dead. I remember thinking that the winner of this contest should be the person who could actually sleep while the choir of nasal kazoo players slept.

When I could stand the noise no longer, I walked out to the ball diamond. After watching the country kids play ball, I was glad that I was ready to play Little League baseball in the city. I watched as they played and I chuckled at their errors and clumsy styles of throwing the ball. I'm so glad that my dad and friends at school played catch with me. I certainly could throw and catch better than any of them.

About two in the afternoon, most of the men arrived at the ball diamond. They were gentlemen because they didn't start the game until the women had cleaned up the eating area. Suddenly, remembering that my Black Diamond baseball glove and runners that were in the Fargo, I ran as fast as I could because I didn't want to miss a chance to play ball with the men.

A short balding fellow yelled, "Anyone wanting to play ball, stand by the backstop. The only rule is that no kids are allowed to play, unless they are in their teens. We'll play a game with them later. Hurry! Everyone line up so we can choose teams."

My heart sank because I wasn't old enough to play but suddenly I felt a hand on my shoulder. I looked up and there was Cliff.

"Stay with me, kid. When I'm picked I'll tell them that I want to have this young man play beside me, since he can throw the ball for me 'cause of my sore shoulder."

A tall man, named Hilbert, and a heavy-set man, named Solly had the difficulty of selecting the teams. One by one, men were being selected, when suddenly I heard Cliff's name.

He stepped forward and pulled me to his side. "Since my shoulder is still sore, I need someone to throw the ball for me, so I want Mabel's nephew to come with me."

No one seemed to mind, so we stood behind Solly because we were on his team. Then I noticed that none of these men had baseball gloves.

"How are they going to catch the ball?" I whispered to Cliff "because they don't have no gloves."

He leaned over, "Just watch. They're here for the fun of it

and some of them may just surprise you. 'Sides they don't need no gloves to play."

Aunt Mabel overheard our conversation and closed her eyes and shook her head.

Cliff and I stood in center field for three innings and not one ball came to us, but I did see some of the men catch the ball with their bare hands. Throwing was easy for most of them, but catching the ball was a different story. Half way through the third inning a lady called, "Cliff, you're the next batter." Cliff nudged me. "You bat for me," he said. "They won't mind."

All of the bats were notched, chipped and two were cracked and heavily taped. I grabbed one that I thought was a sure thing and stepped to the plate.

Aunt Mabel cheered as I scratched my feet in the dirt to get a better place to stand. The pitcher had a large round stomach, a handlebar moustache and a hole in the knee of his pants.

"Take it easy on him, Willy. He a young city kid," yelled Cliff.

Willy nodded and spit onto the ball and then stepped up to pitch.

The first pitch arched slightly, making it easy to time my swing. I swung with all my might and missed. Aunt Mabel shouted, "Come son. Take the next one and show your worth!"

The second pitched arched and I swung again.

"This bat's too heavy," I said as I started for the stack of weather beaten bats.

"It's the lightest one we got," yelled Solly as he waved his hand. "Just choke up a little. You'll be alright."

The next ball arched toward me and I connected, driving the ball out into right field. It was along the right field base line, so it took some time for the old gray haired man to get to the ball. By the time he reached it, I was on second and heading for third.

The crowd was cheering and I heard someone yell, "RUN! RUN YOU LITTLE BAST ... AH KID! GO FOR HOME! YOU CAN MAKE IT." It was Cliff.

I rounded third base and saw Cliff waving his sore arm. As I neared home plate, I heard the ball bounce near me so I decided to slide. When the dust settled, I was safe but the right knee of my pants had a large hole in it.

The crowd cheered and my Aunt ran out on to the field and hugged me in front of everyone, then she limped back to her seat, holding her ribs. Our team was ahead, four to three.

The next time I went to bat, the pitcher was ready. He tossed the ball past me before I was ready. He certainly had less pity on me than the first time.

Cliff yelled, "Come on, Willie. He's still young'un, so pitch a little slower!"

I grounded it back to Willie and was out on first but felt good because I had hit the ball.

In the bottom of the ninth inning a fly ball finally made its way to center field. Cliff called to me, "It's your ball, Kid! Show them how to catch it."

My eye was on the ball as I started to back up. It was one of the highest balls that I had ever tried to catch. The sun overhead smiled on me as I confidently planted both legs to catch the ball. Suddenly, my footing seemed unsteady and I started to fall. Every attempt to correct my position was futile. I ended up leaning to my right and the ball struck my glove as my knee hit the ground and that is when the ball found its way out of the mesh and rolled onto the ground.

I heard the crowd cheer. In terror, I searched for the ball but

Cliff picked it up, then leaned back and threw the ball almost all the way to home plate. It bounced once and the catcher tagged the hitter just moments before he crossed the plate.

"**OUT!**" shouted Mr. Keller.

"Sorry, Cliff. I thought I had it but my footing, I … I …"

"You slipped on some fresh cow shh … I mean manure, so now you have a hole in one knee and manure on the other knee. I must say you're one hell of a ball player."

"But your shoulder? Is it OK?"

"By the way that's known as teamwork. 'Sides, who'll remember, 'cause the game's over?"

"Won't anyone complain?" I asked hoping that he would say no.

"What's to complain? The fresh cow sh … ah manure made you miss the ball and besides you would have caught it anyway. Wouldn't yah?"

"Ah … sure," I said as we walked toward the backstop, not sure if I should be embarrassed or pleased that we won the game.

Aunt Mabel came out to hug me again but when she saw the manure on my pants she stepped back and laughed. "I thought you had it covered, but I see it covered you."

Cliff laughed and I felt like a fool until he said, "Great hit. We won seven to six and it was your home run that helped us win."

The smell on my pant leg was terrible even though I washed it at the horse trough. I decided to ride in the back of the Fargo all the way home. Besides, I didn't want to be sitting in the cab when Cliff put his arm around Aunt Mabel. I always felt happy for them but … I felt as if I should not be there when they were so close to each other.

CHAPTER 10

THE OUTHOUSE AUCTION

The rain fell continuously for three days. Much of my time was spent on the porch reading Hardy Boys books and eating homemade cookies. It was so nice to have Fritz near me. He seemed to be doing better and adjusting to losing his eyesight in the one eye. Often, he would come over to me and nudge me, as if to ask for a hug and a cookie. I admit that he did get his share of cookies. Oh, I had chores to do but I managed to eat my share of cookies too. I had chickens to feed and garbage to carry out, but most of my time was spent on the porch.

On the third day, Cliff arrived and just as he closed the door of his truck there was a sudden downpour. He arrived on the porch rather soaked and with mud on his boots. After shaking off the excess water on his jacket and hat, he removed his boots and smiled at me.

"At least you don't have to shovel it like snow. BRRRR ... it is rather chilly."

Aunt Mabel stepped onto the porch. She always seemed to know when he would arrive. She put her hand on his forearm and he smiled at me as he put his arm around her shoulder.

"Coffee on?" he asked as he glanced at the plate with only two cookies on it.

"Sure thing," she said as she turned and went into the house.

"Well," he said as he pulled up his favorite chair and reached for his pipe. "I see that you're having a tough day."

"Naw. The Hardy Boys books are good stories and the cookies are even better. This rain gives me time to rest up from the hard work."

"Well this afternoon we're off to an auction sale near Rocky Mountain House. I heard that ..."

Just then Aunt Mabel arrived with Cliff's favorite cup and it was filled to the brim with strong coffee. I could smell it from where I was sitting. "You heard what?" she asked as she handed him the coffee.

"There's an auction near Rocky Mountain House and I heard from Frank Cubberstaad that there will be at least five young bulls for sale. I thought that since you needed a bull, maybe we could go and see what's available."

"What time does it start?" she asked.

"Some time after lunch."

"Sure. Let's finish our coffee and then we'll go."

There was only one chapter left to read in the Hardy Boys book, The Secret of Skull Mountain but Aunt Mabel and Cliff were ready to go, so I set the book on my chair, pulled on my boots, grabbed my jacket and ran to the truck.

Cliff stopped at his place and hitched up his stock trailer. "This is just in case she decides to buy a bull," he said as we checked the tires before stepping back into the truck.

"Besides the rain will wash off all of the cow manure, right?" I teased.

"Maybe it's the manure that holds it together," Aunt Mabel said as she grabbed Cliff's arm.

We drove for an hour on roads that were very muddy and slippery. Cliff and Aunt Mabel talked constantly to each other: barely letting me into the conversation so I sat quietly, regretting that I hadn't brought my book.

The rain stopped when we crossed James River. Several miles away the road was dry and it appeared as if it had not rained there at all. In fact, when we arrived at the farm site where the auction sale was, it was dry and sunny. Many trucks were parked under trees and all of them were parked in as many different directions as there were trucks. None of them were in line or in any order.

The auction sale had already started and many of the smaller items had been sold, but the auctioneer encouraged the crowd to follow him over to the farm machinery.

"I've been to a few auction sales before and they're fun," I said as I looked over at Cliff.

"Just remember not to wave your hand and tip your hat or the auctioneer will think you are interested in buying and will call your bid," warned Aunt Mabel.

Two cultivators, a drill press, a hay wagon and two sets of harrows were the first pieces of farm machinery for sale. The next items to be sold were an old faded McCormick Derring tractor, a hay rake and a faded baler with a flat tire. I was most interested in the grain auger. It was like the one that my friend's father owned on his grain farm in Saskatchewan.

"The McCormick Derring tractor was one of the first built in 1933. It's old but it runs," said Cliff. "He's got a new tractor, a 1952 McCormick Derring Model W4 so now he plans to sell the old one."

Just then I heard the auctioneer say, "Someone has asked if the old outhouse is for sale." Everyone laughed. "So ... just before we go to the corrals to sell the cattle, we'll auction off the old outhouse. I've never auctioned off an outhouse before but since two people have asked about it, let's see who wants it, OR should I say who needs it?"

The crowd laughed and several large men with cowboy hats pointed at each other.

The short, rotund auctioneer pointed at the outhouse and started his chatter. "Who needs this old outhouse? It's here for the buying, so who'll give me five dollars?"

Before he could begin his auctioneering rhythmic chatter, an old man with a long tattered beard held up two fingers and said, "I'll give yah a coupla bucks."

"I've got a two dollars bid, two dollars yah hear: two dollar bid and two makes four. Who'll give me four? Four dollars: four, four abid abid four. What about four? How about a four dollar bid? Who has a four dollar bill in his pocket?"

"Yes!" shouted his auction partner that stood on the back of a small truck to scan the crowd for bids.

"We've got a four now a five? Five, fi fi fi five abid fi five: how about it, folks? What about five dollars bid? I've got a bid for four, how about a five? If you guys think you need it or could use it on some cold night, or on the way home bid five. It's here or Eli Stootgaard gets it. You bid a four. How about a five? Fi, fi fi, five: who'll bid five? What about a five dollar bid?"

Suddenly, he pointed to the back and yelled, "**YES!**"

"I see that five dollar bid. I've got a five, how about seven or seven and a half? I've got five Eli, so you'd better bid or you'll have to pay to use it."

Again the crowd laughed and the auctioneer continued his chatter and soon had the price up to ten dollars. Eli seemed confident that outhouse was his, for the lively auctioneer was starting the count down. "Going once; twice: any last bids?" There was a small pause.

A man beside me raised his hand and yelled, "**ELEVEN DOLLARS!**"

"My goodness, this outhouse is bringing more money than the old seeder that we just sold. I guess work is an option but going to the outhouse ain't." The auctioneer paused to wipe his mouth with the back of his hand when someone shouted, "**ELEVEN!**"

"Hey, we already have an eleven dollar bid. What about twelve? It's only one dollar more. One hundred cents so if you have any sense, give me a twelve dollar bid, Eli. How about it? Will you give twelve dollars for an outhouse that has been broken in and ready for use? You'd better buy it or you'll have to hide in the ditch on the way home."

Eli nodded and suddenly the outhouse was up to twelve dollars.

Someone in the crowd shouted, "Does that price include paper?"

The auctioneer shouted back, "I only sell 'em, I don't supply what's in em. Now let me hear another bid. Someone open the door and let everyone see how nice and comfortable that outhouse is." As he took a drink of water, someone went to the door of the outhouse and pulled on the door. It was stuck, so he pulled as hard as he could but the door still did not budge.

"IT'S STUCK," he shouted to the auctioneer.

"Probably needs a small adjustment or just another farm to sit on. Any last bids before we move on? We've got a twelve dollar bid for a well used or should I say an experienced outhouse."

A woman with a straw hat shouted, **"THIRTEEN DOLLARS!"**

Maybe I should give up auctioneering and go into selling old outhouses," said the auctioneer.

Again the crowd laughed.

I looked at the guy beside me and he did not move a muscle but somehow the auctioneer saw his bid.

"Thank you Sir. I now have fourteen dollars. Now we're getting serious. Is there anyone else who wants to bid on this outhouse? How about fifteen? Fifteen, fifteen: what about fifteen bid. Do I hear fifteen?"

"Fifteen, fif, fif, fif, fifteen, let's go. Fifteen is only seven two dollar bills and four quarters or two seven dollar bills and a dollar. Better hurry. What about you, Eli?"

Eli closed his eyes and shook his head, in disappointment.

"Last call for the outhouse. I've got a fourteen dollar bid and fifteen will take it unless you get in now. How about it? An outhouse with character for only fifteen dollars. The wood costs more than that. The door may need some adjustments but the seat is comfortable. I've got fourteen dollars on it but do I hear fifteen?"

There was a momentary pause.

"YES!" shouted the auctioneer's partner. "Fifteen, over here."

"We've got a bid at fifteen so why miss out on this steal of a deal? Give sixteen. It's now or never," called the rotund auctioneer.

"SIXTEEN!" a voice in the crowd called and every head turned.

"Thank you. Why fool around with a dollar at a time let's hear a twenty dollar bid? Twenty, twen, twen and a twenty. How about a twenty bid and some paper will be thrown in? Think about it, ready for use and ready for you to go. All you need is twenty dollars. Think about it, you can even use it on the way home."

The man, who stood beside me, twitched ever so slightly and then the auctioneer shouted, "**TWENTY DOLLARS!** I've got a bid of twenty dollars. Any more bids?"

No one moved and that was the end of the bidding.

"**SOLD!**" shouted the auctioneer as he pointed to the man beside me.

"What are you going to do with it?" someone asked and he replied, "We'll take it to the church camp at Gull Lake. They need more outhouses there. I hate standing in line when I'm at camp."

"Paint your name on it and it will be your personal place," taunted a gray haired man with no teeth.

The crowd laughed as they moved over to an old green International truck but as the Auctioneer was about to begin his chatter, someone in the crowd called, "HEY, ELMER. You may have sold an outhouse but a lady just stepped out of it. Does she come with it?"

The crowd laughed as the poor lady quickly moved to hide behind a granary, out of public view. That is when I recognized the lady; it was Aunt Mabel.

As the crowd's laughing subsided, the auctioneer called, "Say Eli, you should have bid a few dollars more then you could have bought a wife with that outhouse. You wouldn't have to live alone this winter."

Eli shook his head as I ran to the rear of the granary to see if Aunt Mabel was OK.

"Are you alright?" I whispered.

"Yes, just embarrassed. Who'd think that using an outhouse at an auction sale could be so embarrassing?"

"Aw, come on. Let's sneak around to the back of the farmhouse so we can get away from the crowd."

Once the crowd moved to the next item for sale, we moved to the back of the buyers so no one could see us, Cliff came over and nudged Aunt Mabel. "Well that's one way to become popular."

She elbowed him and I laughed out loud.

"He did get 20 dollars for that old outhouse," said Aunt Mabel.

"Twenty bucks, why that's a hell of a price for an outhouse. Maybe I should start building some and taking them to Elmer's auctions," said Cliff.

When we arrived at the corral the auctioneer climbed to the top rail. "Have a look at these bulls. Any one of these bulls will be a good investment. They've all been dehorned and are healthy, so there's nothing to worry about."

"Let's start with the black one in the corner. How about the one with the white star on his forehead? Who will give me a strong bid for this Angus bull?"

As he started his chatter, Cliff turned to Aunt Mabel. "None of these bulls are that great. There is only one Hereford and it's rather small. Unless you get it for a decent price, I wouldn't bother with any of them," he said.

I watched how bidders would nod their heads or move their index fingers. One man tipped his hat and one man rubbed his nose. It was so subtle that the untrained eye would likely miss it. Two bulls were sold and when the auctioneer announced that the brown and white Hereford was next, Cliff leaned over to Aunt Mabel and said, "Let's open up the bid and see where it goes."

"Here's a bull that is a bit smaller but I'm sure that he will make some profits. He's been dehorned and had his shots and is ready to visit your pasture, so do we have a bid?"

Cliff shouted, "**TEN DOLLARS!**"

"Ten dollars? This bull is worth much more than that. Even if you cut him up for steaks and roasts, you'd get more.

"**TEN DOLLARS!**" called Cliff.

"Well a bid is a bid. You fellas are making me work hard for my money," said the auctioneer as a voice in the crowd called, "**FIFTEEN DOLLARS!**"

The auctioneer went on, "I've got fifteen dollars so who will give me twenty. Twenty, twenty, how about twenty for this young Hereford? Come on folks have a look."

Cliff leaned over and whispered to me, "Bid twenty."

I placed my foot on the bottom rail of the corral and adjusted my hat so I could have a better look and then flipped my wrist when the auctioneer was looking in my direction.

"HEY! I've got a twenty dollar bid from a young fella over there. You men had better have another look at this bull or this young man will get the best buy of all. How about twenty-five dollars? Who will go for twenty-five? Twenty five, twenty five, five five five, twenty five."

In a few moments, the bid was up to thirty-five dollars. Cliff nudged me and I flicked my wrist and the auctioneer shouted, "Hey, **FORTY DOLLARS**! Who will go forty-five, forty-five, I say, how about forty-five? Do I hear forty-five?"

On the other side of the corral, a tall man in a black hat

nodded his head and the auctioneer shouted, "**FORTY-FIVE DOLLARS**. I knew this one was too good to be sold for such a low price. How about fifty? Anyone for a fifty dollar bid? Fifty dollars, fifty, fifty, I say fifty."

There was a pause and he resumed, "Well, if you don't like fifty how about forty-seven and a half. Let's have forty-seven and a half."

Cliff nudged me, so I flicked my wrist.

Again the auctioneer yelled, "**YES**" and pointed at me.

"Fellas, I've got a forty-seven and a half bid from this young rancher. He knows his beef and he's about to buy a good bull. If he thinks that it's worth that kind of money you'd better have another look. Let's have fifty. I need fifty. Do I have a fifty dollar bid, anywhere? Fifty, fifty, fifty."

"**YES**! The auctioneer shouted. "I've got a bid from over here. Fifty dollars is a good buy. No sense missing out on a good thing. Let's go to fifty-five. Do I have someone with fifty-five dollars in their pocket for a good Hereford bull?"

As he chattered, Cliff whispered, "Nope. Don't bid. It's too high."

I looked at him with disappointment. "Really? But this is fun."

"It's too much and the last one is not worth much so let's go and find your Aunt Mabel. She is probably having a coffee somewhere."

"I thought she was here with us," I said as I looked around.

"She left us to sit down somewhere 'cause she's is not feelin' well," said Cliff.

Walking back to the coffee stand, we saw her visiting with two ladies. When we approached, she excused herself and started to walk toward us and I noticed that she was limping. When she joined us, I reached over to offer my arm and she hung on as we walked to the Fargo.

"Sorry, Mabel. No bulls or anything to take home," said Cliff.

"That's OK. No need to buy someone else's problems," she replied.

When we reached the main road, Cliff shifted to fourth gear and we drove several miles in companionable silence.

"You know Mabel, I sure would have missed you had you been sold with that outhouse," Cliff said as he leaned forward and looked at me.

I smiled even though I wasn't sure what Aunt Mabel would say.

"If I'd known that you would have come along with that rickety outhouse, I'd have bid it up to at least, say one hundred dollars," he continued.

Innocently, I replied, "I'd have bid more. She's worth it and you know it."

"Yah, you're right," laughed Cliff, "at least five or ten dollars more."

Aunt Mabel gave a long sigh. "That was the most embarrassing thing that has happened to me in a long time. Imagine the chance of being caught in an outhouse while it's being sold."

"That old man looked rather disappointed. Didn't he?" asked Cliff as he winked at me.

"Sure did," I replied.

"Both of you would have missed me, had he taken me," she said.

Cliff put his arm around her, and I turned away to look out of the passenger side window of the Fargo.

CHAPTER 11

THE HOOK IN THE EAR

It had been a long day and I was tired. We had a wonderful supper and eventually found our favorite chairs on the porch as the sun disappeared over the fir trees near Deadwood Creek. Fritz lay beside me and my hand reached down to scratch his ears.

Cliff put his cup on the rail of the porch and looked at me. "I think that all of us need to go fishing. What do yah think?"

I looked at Aunt Mabel and she shrugged her shoulders.

"That would be just great. When and where do we go?" I asked as I stood to my feet.

"The best fishin' this time of the year is in Ram River country. We could go up to the falls but anywhere along the river is great." He stirred the ashes in his pipe as he spoke.

"When should we go?" asked Aunt Mabel.

"Let's go tomorrow," I said. "What do I need?"

"I have all of the fishin' gear we need. Mabel, all you have to do is bring some of your fried chicken, potatoes and a fresh pie."

"That sounds like more work than the fish are worth," she said as she opened the screen door and went inside for more coffee.

After a half-hour of planning, we all agreed that we would go the day after tomorrow. To me, that seemed too far away.

Expectations were high and I barely slept that night. I had not been fishing since Mr. Janke and Mr. Haag took all the boys in their Sunday School class to Lake Newell near the town of Brooks in Alberta.

I spent most of the next day hoeing the garden and when I painted the outhouse, I laughed because it reminded me of Aunt Mabel and the outhouse at the auction sale. Aunt Mabel prepared chicken, baked bread and made a berry pie. That evening, I went to bed early and anxiously waited for the morning.

The next morning when I heard my name, I was out of bed, dressed and in the kitchen in a matter of minutes. I chose not to make my bed but Aunt Mabel reminded me to be sure that my room was in order before I ate breakfast.

"Before you get into too much of a rush, I need to tell you that Bessy has not been milked this morning, so please hurry 'cause the pancakes will be ready in about twenty minutes," she said as she opened the oven door.

As I closed the screen door of the house, Cliff drove into the yard.

"Well, are you awake this time of the mornin'?" he asked as he slammed the door of his truck.

"Sure am," I said as I started for the barn with the milk bucket in my hand. "All I have to do is milk Bessy, and I'll be back for breakfast."

I herded her into the barn and she went directly to her stall.

I grabbed the milk stool and began to milk as fast as I could. Next to me four cats meowed, hoping that I would squirt some fresh milk their way. By now I was becoming a pretty good milker and Bessy didn't seem to mind.

After breakfast, all of us helped Aunt Mabel do the dishes and soon we were off to Ram River. On the way, Cliff bragged about the fish he had caught and the prize elk he had hunted in that area. It seemed like such a perfect spot.

When we arrived, the sun was relatively high and so were our spirits. It took some effort but we managed to carry the fishing poles, hooks and all of the food about half a mile to the ideal spot that Cliff had spoken about. Along the way, he pointed out places, where most of the fish had been caught last time and he even showed where he had shot one of his largest elk.

The day was perfect. Could anything possibly go wrong?

Cliff tied a hook onto Aunt Mabel's fishing line and showed her where to fish, so she wandered off to the sandy shoreline and started to cast the hook into the stream. Once Cliff saw that she was fishing, he placed a hook on my fishing line and then told me how to fish in these waters.

"You have to toss the hook gently upstream. Distance is not necessary. Look for an area where the water is a little deeper than normal. If the hook moves past you because the stream carries it, wait a few moments, reel it in and then toss it back up stream again. It will take patience but trust me, the fish are here."

As I started to walk up stream, he called to me, "Don't go too far. I want to know where you are at all times."

I waved my hand and didn't look back but continued walking. When I found what I thought to be the ideal place, I stepped down to the shoreline and cast the line into the fast running-water. I could see fish in the water and I hoped that one of them would take my hook. It would be great to catch the first big fish, especially the biggest one of the day. After six casts, no fish seemed interested in my hook.

Half-an-hour later, I moved farther up stream to a more ideal spot. Here I had the opportunity to stand on a log and cast the hook farther into the river. An hour later, still no bites, so I decided to move toward a beaver dam I could see some distance away.

Occasionally, several mosquitoes bothered me but this morning was too perfect for a few mosquitoes to ruin it. Still no bites, and yet I could see the fish in the clear, running water.

I wandered off into the bushes to go to the bathroom and returned to the shore next to the beaver dam. As I stood there, I could see several beaver swimming across the stream. It was so nice that I placed my rod on the ground and sat down to watch them.

The early morning sun made me sleepy so I lay back on the log and closed my eyes. I have no idea how long I rested but when I heard Cliff calling, I sat up.

"I'M OK!" I shouted at the top of my voice.

"HAVE YOU HAD ANY LUCK YET?" he yelled.

"NO!"

"WELL LUNCH IS ALMOST READY SO COME BACK IN ABOUT FIFTEEN MINUTES!"

"OK," I shouted as I picked up my rod and tried to cast the hook into the water. It never made it to the water, for it was snagged behind me. Angry at my bad luck, I turned to see which tree I had caught and there to my surprise was a black bear standing on its hind legs with my hook in his ear. Without thinking, I pulled on the line and the bear shook its head and batted at the fishing line.

Again I tugged at the hook and then the bear dropped down on all four legs and started grunting. He shook his head from side to side and then with his front paws swatted at the fishing line.

All of a sudden, I realized that the bear was only twenty feet away from me. I was about to run but before I did, I gave one last hard tug on the line and the bear stood up on his hind legs and growled. He sounded angry so I decided it was time to go for lunch.

I gripped the rod with both hands, placed it on my shoulder, turned and started to run along the shoreline. After a few feet it became difficult to pull the fishing line because the bear had stopped to swat at the hook in his ear. Again he grunted and shook his head from side to side. He was becoming angrier as he started coming toward me. I started to back up and he kept coming towards me but in a slow ambling fashion because he was more concerned about the pain in his ear.

Again I tried to pull on the line but by this time it was entangled in some bushes beside the bear. Hoping that the line would break, I gave it an extra strong pull. Then the bear dropped to the ground and started to roll around.

I watched as he rolled to the edge of the water. When he stopped rolling I decided to give the line an extra tug. Again he stood to his feet and looked at me as if he had just realized that I was the cause of his pain. He made strange noises, swatted at the fishing line, swung his head back and forth from side to side and then started running toward me.

As he charged, I dropped the fishing rod and ran as fast as my cowboy boots could carry me. It was difficult to run because of the rocks, sand and small dead logs that were in my way. Ahead, I could see Cliff and Aunt Mabel sitting on a log and eating dinner.

Cliff saw me coming and stood as I rounded a large tree on the edge of the clearing. "WHAT THE HELL . . ?" he shouted. "RUN BOY, RUN!"

Aunt Mabel tried to run away but Cliff ran toward me. When we met, he picked up a large broken piece of dead wood. He stood between the bear and me as it was still coming toward me.

"HEAD FOR THE TRUCK!" Cliff yelled, "AND LEAVE THE FOOD. HE'LL STOP WHEN HE SMELLS THE FOOD. JUST KEEP RUNNING!"

I remember Aunt Mabel stumbling ahead of me and at one point I looked back and saw that the bear had stopped by the food. Cliff moved toward the campfire and the bear looked up at him, moved his head from side to side and grunted loudly.

Cliff shouted at him as the bear started to eat some of the food. He knocked over the picnic basket and stepped into the pie.

I returned so that I had a better view of Cliff and the bear. Aunt Mabel shouted at me to stay away, but I inched forward for a better view. In the bright sunshine, I could see a shiny fishing line leading up to the bear's ear but the bear seemed to be more interested in the food, particularly the pie that was now all over his foot.

After licking the pie from his paw, he walked slowly toward Cliff, who was standing by the campfire. The bear was making loud noises and swaying its head back and forth from side to side and at one point he began to wave his front paw in Cliff's direction.

Once the bear arrived next to the small fire, he stopped and looked at Cliff who was standing on the opposite side of the fire. Cliff had a large piece of deadwood in his hand and seemed so sure of himself.

When I was about twenty feet from the battle zone, the bear looked over at me and at that moment, Cliff reached down to the campfire and took a large pot of boiling water and threw it into the face of the bear.

The bear dropped to the ground and grunted loudly as he tried to wipe the hot water off his face. Cliff stepped closer and hit the bear with the large dead branch of wood he was carrying.

The loud crack of the wood striking the bear's butt could be heard from where I was standing. In an instant, the bear turned and started to run toward the stream. Cliff followed him to the shore and we watched the bear swim across to the other side. In only a matter of a minute or so, he was out of sight.

My legs were too weak to walk so I dropped to one knee and Cliff came over to help me up. "You OK?" he asked.

"I don't know," I managed to whisper. My heart was pounding so hard I thought it would never slow down.

"Look," said Cliff as he pointed to the fishing line on the ground. "You got your fishing line back, but I suspect that you'll never get the hook back. By now that bear is long gone so let's get back to Mabel."

"When we got to the fire, Cliff said, "Let's put out the fire and find her. She's back at the truck."

As the last smoke was rising from the dying fire, Aunt Mabel appeared at the edge of the clearing. She walked over to both of us and took a large breath and put both of her hands on her hips.

"I don't know if there is any chicken left but if there is, let's eat it and get the heck out of here," she said in a rather disgusted tone.

We gathered up the fishing rods, then sat on the log and ate whatever food was left.

"Mabel, you make the best damn chicken in the world," Cliff said as he reached for his pipe, "Even bears like it."

"Well, he liked her pie too," I chimed in.

She smiled and tipped her head to one side, "It's better than fish. 'Sides chickens are a lot easier to catch, clean and cook, aren't they son?" she said.

I hung my head and wrinkled up my nose because I knew that she was teasing me about my fight with the roosters.

"Bears are a little tougher than chickens, but some chickens are pretty tough, aren't they son?" she asked as she smiled at me. I looked away for I well remembered my first day on the ranch.

About an hour later, we were on our way home. Aunt Mabel fell asleep on Cliff's shoulder, and I looked out the right side window of the truck and smiled.

"A little piece of advice," Cliff said as stopped the truck in front of Aunt Mabel's house, "Next time you catch a bear with a fishing line, don't try to reel him in, 'cause they get a bit riled."

"That was a great fishing trip, Cliff," I said as I reached for the fishing rods in the back of the truck.

"May I remind you, Cliff," interrupted Aunt Mabel, "we never caught any fish today? If that was a great fishing trip, please don't invite me along on one of your hunting trips."

"Well the food was good, and Tex caught a bear. I ask you, how often do people catch bears with fishin' line?" He smiled, "You did OK, kid."

"Even the bear did OK. Remember, he got the pie. Well, there's one more in the kitchen, so hurry in," she said as she opened the screen door.

CHAPTER 12

FISTS OF FURY

A couple of days later, while Aunt Mabel and I were having breakfast, Cliff arrived at the ranch, towing his stock trailer. Aunt Mabel asked me if I would go with Cliff to Rocky Mountain House to purchase a bull and I got excited about that, since this assignment would be better than cleaning the chicken coop.

"I'm not feeling well this morning so I will stay home. You guys go ahead."

Cliff drank his coffee on the porch with her as I fed Fritz. I tried not to listen but I overheard him say, "Maybe they will find out what's wrong. Just go. Why not go to the Red Deer Hospital? Both of us will be fine. After all, we survived while you were in the hospital after the black yearling knocked you down. We'll be fine."

I felt uncomfortable overhearing this conversation, so I pretended not to hear. Cliff stood, picked up his hat and started for his truck. We left the farm and he said nothing for the first few miles.

"Am I too young to know if anything is wrong?" I asked in an apologetic tone.

"Aunt Mabel doesn't feel well. That's all," he said as he shifted into fourth gear. "Worries me some, that's all."

I didn't ask any more questions but sat in silence.

Twenty minutes later I turned to Cliff, "What kind of bull do we need?"

"Well," he said as he tipped back his hat, "Mabel needs a replacement for the one she shot and that's what we plan to do today. We're off to Herb Babich's ranch. Herb has several bulls that he plans to sell and he's always got pretty good stock."

We drove in silence and my mind wrestled with Aunt Mabel's health. I did recall that she had been in some discomfort for days but never asked her about it. Another half hour passed before we turned onto a rather nice highway and drove in a westerly direction. Cliff stared at the road as he smoked his pipe.

Hungry for conversation, I looked over at him. "I don't know much about bulls. I don't know how to judge 'em. How do you know which one to choose?"

Well," he said as he removed his hat and placed it on the seat between us. "First you look at their size, the way they stand, the size of their private parts and ... things like that."

"Oh," I said as if satisfied with his answer.

"Their legs and shoulder should be strong and square, and their spine straight, of course. And they should come from a good line of cattle," he continued.

"What's a line?"

"They should have a good strong father and a mother which are good beef cattle. When you stand next to them you should not hear them wheezing as they breath and their hooves should be healthy."

Soon we turned down a road that led under a ranch post with the head of a moose. Below the head was written, Lakeview Ranch. As we neared the buildings, I could see three young boys running out of a grove of trees on the north side of the buildings.

"Your job is to stay with the truck at all cost. Keep those hellions from my truck. Last time I was here, they drained some gas from my tank, let air out of my tires and put grease on the steering wheel." He shifted down and brought the truck to a stop, near the barn. As he opened his door, he looked at me, "Remember to do whatever you have to, to keep this truck free from those little rotten bast ... I mean kids!" Then he winked and the corner of his mouth turned up. "I know you can do it. This is city stuff and you can handle it."

Cliff walked over to the barn and was soon joined by a man with a short scruffy beard. He was short and very wide at the shoulders and he wore a straw hat. Both of them disappeared into the large pen where the bulls were. I decided to step outside the truck to see where the three boys were. One was about my age and the others were a lot younger.

I leaned against the grill of the truck and tipped my hat back as I watched them approaching. Unsure of what my next move would be, I put on my leather gloves and spit into the palms and rubbed them together. When I did, the three of them stopped and looked at me.

Just then their black and white dog walked up to me and wagged his tail. I reached down to scratch his ears and when I did, the oldest boy yelled at me, "HEY, LEAVE MY DOG ALONE!"

When he said that, I recognized him. He was the one who was fighting with every kid at the community picnic. His hair was uncombed and he had one tooth missing. He looked kinda stupid with pants that were too short for his legs.

He started walking toward me and yelled. "I TOLD YOU TO LEAVE MY DOG ALONE!"

When he was within ten feet of me, I took off my hat and placed it on the hood of Cliff's truck. "You don't have any manners, do you?" I said, hoping that my voice didn't show any fear.

He stopped and looked at his younger brothers and then at me. "I don't like other kids. I like beating them up until they cry."

"Sorry, I don't cry. Not even after a fight," I said as I tugged on the cuffs of my leather gloves.

He stood several arms lengths away from me and stared at me. At that moment, his dog left my side and wandered off toward the house. I cast a quick glance toward the cattle pens, where Cliff had gone, but I didn't see him.

"You look stupid with them leather gloves," he said, taunting me.

I squared my shoulders and made sure that I was showing no signs of fear.

"My job is to keep all of you from this truck and I will do that. I'm not looking for a fight but if you decide to start one, I'll finish it," I said as I could feel my heart beating in my chest.

He kicked some dirt toward me and in a moment my fighting experience from Earl Kitchener Elementary Grade School paid off. I jumped at him and kicked him in the shin and he dropped to one knee in pain. I made the biggest fist I could muster and swung it upward at his jaw and he went down on the ground with a loud groan.

Instantly, his two brothers started running toward the

farmhouse, so I stepped back to the truck. "I never started this fight. 'Sides, my job is to keep you from this truck. Come near and I'll make you sorrier than you are now." My cheeks felt very hot.

He moaned for a few moments, staggered to his feet and limped rapidly toward the farmhouse. I had the feeling that he would be back, so I opened the driver's side of Cliff's truck and looked for something to help me, should he return. There to my surprise was an old worn out broom. I grabbed it and put it beside me as I sat on the front bumper and watched the farmhouse.

Cliff was not returning, so I walked to the back of the trailer to have a pee and there to my surprise were the three boys, standing about fifteen feet away. They started throwing rocks and me. As I tried to get out of the way but one rock struck my left arm. The pain was terrible. It must have been a sharp rock. I realized that this wasn't a game, so I started running toward them, with the broom in my hand. This kept them from throwing more rocks.

They started to run in three different directions and I knew that I could not catch all of them and guard the truck at the same time. I watched as the middle-aged boy ran to the outhouse and closed the door, so I followed him and closed the latch on the outside. I knew that he would not be back for some time.

The youngest ran into the house and locked the screen door. To my right, I could see the eldest boy running into the grove of trees, so I followed. If it were not for the crackling of some branches, I wouldn't have known where he was. I saw him briefly behind a tree and then I looked up and there he was climbing up a ladder to a tree house that looked like a fort. From there, he was able to throw rocks at me. It was like being in the Crusades, where knights attacked castles. He seemed to have an endless supply of objects and I knew that I had to find cover or flee.

Behind the tree that he was in, I noticed the long ladder that he had used to climb into his turret. I moved carefully through the flying rocks until I reached the ladder and then grabbed it and pulled with all my might. The ladder fell to the ground with a loud crash. He was now trapped. This was my finest hour.

Backing out of harm's way, I shouted up at him, "Hope you enjoy the view, 'cause you'll be there for a long time."

I heard some bad words as I ran back to the truck. Cliff and I arrived at the truck at the same time.

"I thought you were guarding my truck," Cliff said as he opened the truck door.

"I am. The kids aren't here are they?"

Cliff drove the truck to the corral and backed it up to load one of the bulls that he had purchased. As Cliff and the other man loaded the young bull into the trailer, I kept my eye on the grove of trees and the outhouse. There was no sign of life at either.

"Say, you're a nice young lad. You should meet my kids," said the man with the scruffy beard. "They're about your age. They're probably in their tree house in that stand of trees behind the house. You should go and see if you can find them."

"I'll meet them some other time," I managed to say as I looked at Cliff.

"They don't get out much, so it would be nice for you to meet them," the man continued, unaware of where his children were or what had happened to them.

"Mabel will put the cheque for the bull in your mail box in

town. Right now, she is not feeling up to being here," apologized Cliff.

We started down the road and as we turned onto the main road, Cliff looked over at me, "Did you meet the little bast … ah… I mean little troublemakers?"

I rolled down the window to allow fresh air to blow over my warm face. "Yep, and they'll remember me."

"I noticed that when I came back from the corral you were carrying my broom; the one that is usually under the seat of my truck. Did yah have to use it?"

"Kinda."

It was good to hear Cliff laugh. All the way to the Broken Antler Ranch, he chuckled at what I told him about our meeting. It seemed to take his mind off Aunt Mabel.

We unloaded the Hereford bull into Aunt Mabel's corral and watched as he walked around sniffing the air. His coat was shiny and the white hair on his face seemed very clean.

"I think Aunt Mabel will like him," I said.

"He's the best I've seen in a long time," replied Cliff.

"When will she be back?"

"In a few hours, I suppose. I think that she went to Red Deer Hospital and that's quite a long drive. I shoulda gone with her."

Later that evening, we sat on the porch as Cliff smoked his pipe. Aunt Mabel came home quite late and by the time she arrived, Cliff had supper ready. We ate together and it was a wonderful evening. When the moon appeared on the horizon, we went outside and sat on the porch.

"So what did you do besides buy a bull?" she asked.

"Well, sonny boy was very helpful today," chuckled Cliff as lit his pipe.

"Did you meet Herb Babich's boys?" she asked as she sipped on her coffee.

"He sure did," responded Cliff as he took his pipe into his mouth. He paused as he exhaled smoke, "Those three little bast ... ah I mean kids of Herb's need someone to teach them manners and to keep them in line."

"Yes, I heard that they're trouble at school, too," she said just before going into the house for more coffee.

At ten o'clock, Cliff and Aunt Mabel walked to his truck. She leaned against the fender of the truck as he put his foot on the running board. They talked for a long time before Cliff opened the truck door.

Before getting in and driving away, he yelled at me, "Thanks, kid. You can ride with me anytime."

That was the nicest thing anyone had ever said to me.

CHAPTER 13

THE HOLE THING

A few days later, Cliff, Aunt Mabel and I went to another town for another rodeo. After finding a place to park the Fargo, we started for the Grandstand to purchase tickets for the afternoon show.

Looking toward the infield, I saw a tractor pulling harrows and behind it a second tractor was pulling a large log to level the ground for the riders for the afternoon rodeo. Dozens of cowboys were standing around, some playing with lariats and some brushing their horse's manes. Occasionally one would spit onto the ground as they spoke to each other. Most of them smoked 'roll your own' cigarettes that hung at unusual angles from their lips. They looked so tough that I vowed again that when I was old enough to smoke, I would try a pipe first and then cigarettes like theirs. That seemed so neat that I practiced spitting every day.

Off in the distance, I could hear several calves calling to their mothers and behind the Grandstand, music was playing for some mechanical rides like the Ferris Wheel and Roller Coaster.

I tipped my hat to the side so it looked like Cliff's, and cast a glance over the crowd. Hundreds of people were busy eating, visiting and preparing for the afternoon show to begin. Aunt Mabel placed a pillow under her when she sat down 'cause it was likely more comfortable than sitting on the hard wooden planks. Cliff stood nearby and talked with several cowboys as I shoved my hands into my pockets like he did and looked back toward the infield.

"Will there be any calf riding?" I casually asked the lady beside me.

"Usually is. Why? Do you ride?" she asked.

"Yes, I brought my chaps and gloves," I said with confidence as I looked her straight in the eye.

She smiled. "Do you practice much?" she asked.

"I won the Calf Riding Contest in Rocky Mountain House last month."

"Really? How long have you been riding?" she asked as her face lit up.

"Well," I said as I pulled up my pants and adjusted my hat, "it doesn't matter how long you have been riding as long as you can ride the full eight seconds and win. That's what counts."

"My husband, Fred, is at the back of the chutes. Do you see him? He's the one wearing the red shirt, over next to the rodeo clowns." She seemed proud to point him out to me. I felt like a celebrity.

"Yah," I said as I wiped my mouth with the back of my hand.

"If you want to ride, you should talk to him. Tell him that you spoke to his wife. By the way, I'm Elma. If there's still room on the afternoon riding list, he'll do what he can to let you ride."

"Really?"

She smiled and I turned and looked up at Cliff. He smiled,

"Your chaps and gloves are behind the seat of the Fargo. I'll go with you if you really want to ride again."

My aunt closed her eyes and shook her head. "Are you sure you want to do this again? Maybe you were lucky last time. Remember, that most people hurt fast and heal slow."

Her words couldn't dampen my enthusiasm.

Cliff motioned with his head and both of us started for the truck. After picking up my chaps and gloves, we rushed to the back of the chutes. It took us several minutes to find Fred but when we told him that we had spoken to his wife and that I had ridden in the Rocky Mountain House rodeo, he looked at the clipboard in his hand.

"Sorry, there's no room. Ah … no wait … a moment. Yes, we have enough boys riding calves but I need one more rider for the steers. Two riders have dropped out and I could use one. If you're as good as you say you are, well … give me minute." He stepped behind a small booth and returned several minutes later.

"Who will cover your entry fee?"

"I will," said Cliff as he reached into his pocket for his wallet.

The man looked down at me and saw that I was wearing my blue and white chaps. I was hoping that my chaps and gloves would impress him but he just looked at Cliff. "I need two dollars for the entry fee, Cliff."

Cliff handed the two dollars to the man, who gave me a numbered tag to wear on the back of my shirt. The number was #5; my favorite number. What could possibly go wrong?

While Fred was writing down my name, Cliff told him that I had won the Calf Riding event in Rocky Mountain House last month. The man just grunted and pointed to the far end of the chutes. "Be there in twenty minutes."

As Cliff attached the tag to my shirt, he said, "These are

steers and not calves. Steers are bigger, faster and twist more than calves. The fall from them is farther and the seat you sit on is not very nice. It's bony, hard and their skin may shift from side to side: not as much as the bulls, but it shifts around, so be careful."

The next few minutes were a blur. I remember an orchestra playing "Oh Canada" and ladies carrying flags while they were riding their horses. Cowboys were everywhere. One of them, with a large moustache, smiled and patted me on the back. "Good Luck, Shorty," he said. A cold chill went up my spine when I heard his spurs jingle as he walked over to a group of other cowboys.

Cliff tapped me on the shoulder and motioned for me to follow him. We walked between steel fences and stopped by a group of animals. "These are the steers that you'll be ridin'."

"They're quite big aren't they," I managed to whisper.

"They're bigger all right and a lot quicker. Just remember to lean forward when his head comes up and back when it goes down. Oh, and by the way, if he turns, then lean a little into the turn."

"Any thing el ... else?" I stammered.

"Yah, remember to use your knees to keep your balance. These critters are faster, smarter and a lot stronger. You'll have to use all of your limbs to stay on this time."

"That sounds complicated," I mumbled.

"So is falling off."

One of the steers looked at me. He was almost as big and black as the yearling. Suddenly I had second thoughts about my riding career. My mouth was dry and swallowing was difficult.

"I'm kinda dry. I need a drink," I said, trying to take my mind off the task before me.

"Come on," said Cliff. "There's still time to get some lemonade before your ride."

At the lemonade stand, I heard a familiar voice.

"I didn't know that you're a cowboy. You mutht be braver than when you tried to jthump off the diving board at the thurch camp." There to my surprise, was Alva, the black haired girl that called me a thicken, I mean chicken.

Cliff paid for my drink while I sipped on the lemonade. I tried not to look at her but she moved around to stand in front of me.

"Thorry I called you a thicken," she said as she lowered her gaze to my chaps. "It wath mean of me. If I knew that you wasth a rider, I'd have been more careful. Sthorry."

I pulled down my hat and kicked at the ground with my cowboy boots. Just then Cliff tapped me on the shoulder. "Time to go, Tex," he said with a grin.

"Don't drink too much of it or you'll get sick," he said as we walked to the rear of the chutes. Cowboys were getting ready for the bareback riding event and several of them were wrapping their arms with tape.

Before I knew it, the announcer was notifying the crowd that the steer riding event was next. I looked up at Cliff.

"You still can back out, you know. I'll tell Mabel that the steers were big and mean this year. She'll understand."

"But what about Alva?" I asked as I pulled my gloves onto my cold hands.

"One thing you need to know about women is that they are to be liked, helped and respected, but few of them are worth listenin' to and … none are worth dying for."

"But I almost …"

"Yes, I know," he interrupted. "You almost died in that stupid lake for that girl. Who cares if she likes you or doesn't think you're brave? Do your own thing and if it pleases her, then OK and if it doesn't, let her sweat about it."

By now we were standing at the chute I was to ride from and I could hear several cow bells ring, I felt a cold chill go up my spine.

"You're next," said Fred as he passed us.

I climbed up the steel fence and below me was a black and white steer. It was much bigger than the ones Cliff had shown me in the pen. He was as large as the Black Yearling. His head seemed bigger and his back seemed much wider.

"Why do they ... call them ... steers?" I managed to ask as I looked down at the steer.

"Let me put it this way. If you don't ride him then you don't have what he don't have."

"Huh?" His comment made no sense to me, so I just grunted.

"The rope is almost ready," said Cliff.

"He's kinda ... big." I whispered.

"He's larger than any of the others. Maybe he accidentally got into the line of steers. I'd better check before you ride," said Cliff as he jumped down from the fence to speak with Fred.

Someone was wrapping a leather strap around his chest area and putting a rope just in front of his hind legs.

I heard the announcer call my name and I looked for Cliff but he was not there.

"We're waitin' for yah, son so git on and ..." said the man who opens the gate and lets us out into the riding area.

Feeling numb, I put my leg on the gate so I could straddle the beast. As I lowered myself onto his back, Cliff arrived.

"This aint a steer. We'll have to ..." was all I remember hearing him say.

I looked at Cliff. "He's kinda like the … yearling."

"It's your decision, Tex," he said but if you git off we'll get the proper one for you. This ones outta your league. It's a bull."

Fred pointed at me as I gripped the rope. Someone tied it around my fist as the animal bobbed his head. I could feel his ribs moving as he breathed. He seemed so wide that my legs could not get a grip. My hands were now tightly wrapped around the rope. The bull started to move back and forth in the chute and my heart was pounding harder than the day I had jumped off the diving board. His heavy breathing made me think about dying. The only thing I remember thinking was; why am I willing to do this? I'm supposed to grow up and live to be an old man!

Then the black and white beast took several large breaths and I felt his heart beating. Someone pushed my hat down over my ears and my eyes and at that moment the gate opened. The animal's head went down and so did mine but when he raised his head, mine didn't. I heard a loud crack and my forehead felt like a big stick had hit me and my neck felt sore. The top of his head hit my forehead. Suddenly my arms were weak and my shoulders ached. It seemed to me that I heard the crowd cheer as I saw a rodeo clown run in front of me. His face was painted with bright colors and his baggy pants flapped as he ran. A moment later the jerking stopped. My breath was gone and I felt a warm flood of lemonade in the back of my mouth.

Someone rolled me over and I opened my eyes. I felt worse than the day I jumped off the diving board or rode my bicycle into a parked car. My hat was over my eyes, my right leg hurt more than I ever remembered and everything around me was very blurred.

Someone was feeling my arms and legs and then I heard

Cliff's voice. "You're a dang fool, boy! Bright, tough and gamey, but a dang fool."

It was impossible to breathe even though I was gasping for air. It seemed like I was somewhere in eternity. Someone grabbed my legs and bent them to my chest and pumped them up and down. The pain was incredible. Finally breathing became easier. When I sat up, blood flowed down my face onto my shirt and everything I looked at was double. I was sure that I was going to vomit.

Several men carried me off the field and placed me behind the chutes. A First Aid attendant spoke to me as he wiped my forehead with a wet cloth "You don't have any broken bones but your forehead looks like you stopped a truck. Here, lie in the shade and hold this ice on that goose egg on your forehead." He knelt by my side until someone called him and he ran off.

Cliff knelt next to me and held the ice on my forehead. I don't recall how long I lay there but I blinked my eyes and tried to focus on his face. He was talking to me but I did not understand a word he was saying.

I managed to ask, "Did I sssstaaaay on ... long enough?"

"Only long enough to get your head bashed and to get a mouth full of dirt," he replied. "You know, you're tougher than I thought you were. I always thought city kids weren't very tough, but you're OK."

While the crowd cheered, Cliff cleaned the dirt out of my mouth and wiped the dirt off my face. Some time later he helped me sit up. I tried to open my eyes but they didn't want to work so I lay back on the grass.

"You were right," I wheezed. "Steers are tougher, and ... faster and ... higher off the ground."

Cliff wiped my face with the cold wet cloth and somehow I began to feel better. Anything was an improvement.

"Will I live?" I asked, secretly hoping he would say yes.

Cliff helped me to my feet.

I was not sure how long I had been lying there but my legs did not want to work. Cliff had a good grip on me because I was wobbling back and forth.

"I need to stop at the outhouse for a pee," I slurred. I closed my eyes as we shuffled along.

"Well here are the outhouses but you'll have to go in there by yourself," said Cliff. "Sorry but I don't ..."

While we were standing in the line-up, I heard a voice, "Sshay that was thome thsort of ride. You're pretty good even though you fell off." There was a momentary pause, "Can I walk with you?" she said in a coy sort of way. My eyes were blurred, my stomach did not feel well but my heart felt soft and weird when she spoke.

I tried to look up at Cliff but my eyes were still not working very well.

Cliff pushed my hat to the side of my head to hide the goose bump on my forehead. Cliff leaned over to her, "Standing with someone while they're in the line for the outhouse is not lady-like. Why not wait over there by the trash barrel?"

Cliff opened the door of the outhouse and helped me into the outhouse. As I closed the door and turned around, my hat fell from my head, rolled around the seat and fell into the toilet hole. My first instinct was to try to reach it but it rolled to the corner and was out of sight. Unsure of what to do, I stepped out of the toilet and looked for Cliff.

"You're not done yet, are you?" asked Cliff.

"What happened to your thspesial hat?" Alva asked from a distance.

"Ah, well when cowboys have a bad ride, they generally toss their hat away to forget what happened," said Cliff as he reached for me. "Keeping the hat you were using in a bad ride may bring bad luck."

What he said made no sense to me but I nodded in agreement.

"Here you can use mine," I remember him saying as he dropped his large hat on my head.

Looking puzzled, Alva lifted up the brim of Cliff's hat that was far too big on me. "Do they really do that?"

"Sure do," said Cliff with confidence. "If you come back here tonight, after the rodeo, these holes will be full of cowboy hats from those who had bad rides."

"Are you weally telling me the troof?"

"Come back later and stick your head down the hole and check," said Cliff as he tried to lead me to a different outhouse.

When I stepped out of the outhouse sometime later, I felt dizzy but the fresh air was helping to clear my head. My eyes were still blurred but I managed to look at Alva one more time.

She was smiling. "Are you alright?" she asked in a caring way.

"Yea ... and my next ride might be luckier than this one and ... and I won't have to throw away my hat," I mumbled. A moment later, my knees wobbled and I started to lean against Cliff.

"Meet us back here in an hour," said Cliff as he helped me to the Fargo.

I lay on the seat of the truck, while Cliff went to find Aunt Mabel and soon we were on our way home. My head was on Aunt Mabel's lap as we rode for home. It felt like someone had kicked it so I lay as still as I could even though the Fargo bounced over the hundreds of potholes.

Some time later, I managed to sit up, "Cliff. You told Alva to meet us in an hour. How long ago was that?"

"About an hour and a half ago," he said as he slowed the truck for a curve in the road.

"But she'll be waiting for us."

"Waiting is what she should do. Waiting doesn't hurt anyone, especially her," he said as he shifted to fourth gear.

As Aunt Mabel brushed my hair to one side so she could look at the large lump on my forehead. Then she asked "By the way, where is your hat? Did you lose it?"

"I have a spare one at home. With that lump on your head it should fit perfectly … for at least a week." Cliff smiled. "Great kid but a bit thick especially in the head."

"CLIFF," I heard her say.

I wanted to laugh with him but my head hurt too much.

Back at the ranch, I didn't do much more than sit on the porch with Fritz and Aunt Mabel for three days. Little was accomplished, but who cared? After all, it was my summer vacation and all of us needed time to heal.

Cliff's hat fit perfectly and I was glad that my mother didn't see the lump on my forehead.

CHAPTER 14

HOG WILD

Healing was my first priority, but when I limped to the barn to milk Bessy, the cow, I saw Donut standing by the water trough so I walked over to him and rubbed his nose. While I was standing there, I decided that after I had finished milking, I would saddle him and try to ride. It had been some time since I had ridden but today seemed as good as any. Even though I was sore I remember what my uncle said, "Pain is ok 'cause you know it is still workin'."

For the next week, my riding skills were improving to a place where I didn't have to hang onto the saddle horn when Donut was trotting or galloping. My confidence was at an all-time high. Often I felt as if Donut and I were a team. He seemed to know when I wanted to slow down or go faster.

Riding Donut felt so natural by now that on Thursday afternoon, I decided to ride to Cliff's ranch. It was a sunny day and Aunt Mabel was busy doing some baking and housework, so I saddled Donut. The thought that Cliff may not be at home, never did cross my mind, nor did I think about telling Aunt Mabel where I was going.

The first half-mile was uneventful and when I reached the main road, I turned south and rode so that I faced on-coming traffic. That way, Donut and I wouldn't be surprised if a vehicle suddenly came near.

It was a warm day and butterflies would often rise from the ditches and float on the air currents and warm breezes. All I could hear were the sound of Donut's hooves on the dry road and his occasional snorting as he slowly walked toward Cliff's ranch.

Two more miles passed and while I rode, I had time to think about what Aunt Mabel would say when she found out that I had gone without telling her. Somehow, it seemed impossible to return, after all it was as far to go forward as it was to turn around and go back. Besides, if I did, she might not let me go.

A large truck passed us without much difficulty. Donut only lost stride for a moment and snapped his head up but he was manageable. Mile after mile, we traveled and as we neared Cliff's ranch, I wondered what I would do if he was not at home.

I decided that the first thing I would do would be to let Donut have a drink of water and then let him have a well-deserved rest before we returned. Occasionally, I looked up at the sky to see if clouds were forming but the sky was clear, so we continued. We rounded the small lake near Cliff's ranch and I was pleased that I had arrived without any difficulty.

As I neared the entrance to Cliff's ranch, I spotted a large dark animal on the entry road into his yard. It looked like a large horse. I recalled seeing several of his horses and guessed that one of them had escaped from the fenced pasture so I rode on with all the confidence of a seasoned cowboy.

I decided to approach slowly so that I would not frighten the horse. Perhaps it would walk into the yard and then I could put it into the corral. My plan was to move down into the ditch, so the horse was less likely to see us as we neared him. Donut didn't like walking in the ditch but I managed to force him down the steep slope.

When I was near enough to the entrance to the farm yard and the animal, I encouraged Donut to climb out of the ditch by pulling on the reins. He eagerly ran up the side of the ditch and to my surprise it wasn't a horse at all but a large bull moose, like one we had seen a week before down near the slough. The moose was just as surprised to see us as we were to see him. First he moved toward Cliff's ranch, and then he turned to face us.

Donut stopped instantly. I was unsure of what to do next. No one seemed to want to move. I nudged Donut in his ribs with the heels of my cowboy boots and he jumped sideways, unwilling to go forward. The moose started to trot into Cliff's yard and as he ran, he held his head high and continued to sway his large antlers from side to side.

I nudged Donut again and he started trotting behind the moose, which had disappeared behind a grove of trees in the middle of Cliff's yard. Pulling on the reigns to bring Donut to a halt, I looked to the rear of the barn and then toward the house. Cliff was nowhere to be seen, nor was his truck there.

Suddenly, Cliff's two dogs, Tex and Hoss, appeared and started barking as they ran to the rear of the barn. I rode after them and around the haystack. Then I saw both dogs chasing the moose through the yard toward the hog pen. The moose leapt over the wire fence where the hogs were penned and then trotted through their pen, swinging his head from side to side.

The hogs panicked and started to run in different directions.

In a few moments, the moose jumped over the fence at the far end of the pen and disappeared into the forest with the dogs behind him.

The frightened hogs ran into the fence, which collapsed from their weight. Hogs were suddenly running in every direction. Unable to count how many of them there were, I rode to where the fence had collapsed. I jumped off Donut and tried to keep as many of the hogs in the pen. I lifted the wire up to close the gap but had nothing to make it stay there.

Only two hogs were left in the pen. Frantically, I pulled the downed wire and posts until the opening was partially closed. The two hogs eventually walked back to the centre of the pen and grunted loudly as they looked at us.

After I was sure that no more of them would escape, I climbed into the saddle and started to ride out to the back of the ranch, where I had seen the others running. I was glad that Tex and Hoss were not with me or they would have added to the confusion. Apparently, they were still chasing the moose into the forest for I could hear them barking in the trees a long way off.

When I arrived at the back of the farmyard, I entered a clearing that had a long windrow of downed trees that Cliff had pushed there when he was clearing the land. There to my surprise were three hogs walking about. Unsure of how many I needed to find, I decided to herd them back to their pen.

I tied Donut to a post and walk slowly toward the hogs. As I neared them, they turned and looked at me but did not move. Moving to the far right, I walked along the long line of downed trees and then toward them from another angle. All of them started walking back toward the farmyard. A few feet later, they turned and looked at me again. I had the feeling that they were about to bolt for the trees, so I stopped and sat on a log to allow them time to calm down.

Eventually they started toward the farmyard so I followed. That is when I realized that I had a problem. Where was I going to put them? The gate to their pen was closed, the downed wire was high enough to keep them out and there was no other place to corral or hold them.

When I tried to herd them, they would stop, turn and look at me. When I ignored them, they would eventually start walking in the direction of the farmyard. Fortunately, they walked to the pen and stopped while the other hogs in the pen walked over to join them.

Unsure of where to put them, I stopped by the water tank to plan my next move. If I came near, they would run away but if I let them walk around, they might wander off again. I decided to walk back to the clearing and bring Donut into the yard. Maybe the hogs would be calm enough by then that I could lower the fence and eventually encourage them into the pen.

After returning to the farmyard with Donut, I put him into the corral. This would give me more time to try to deal with the hogs. I closed the corral gate and as I walked toward the hogs, I realized that Tex and Hoss were on their way back into the yard. When they spotted the three hogs, the race was on. One of the hogs was so frightened that he pushed his way back into the hog pen and ran toward the hog barn. Each hog started to run with a farm dog in hot pursuit.

Tex chased the larger hog through a garden, across the backyard of the house and into a row of thick trees. Hoss chased the other one out of the yard toward the main roadway. At that moment, I thought I heard Cliff's truck coming into the yard.

The hog that Hoss was chasing was coming my way and I

was sure that I had a chance to stop him, or if not, at least slow him down. I ran across the hog's pathway, planted my feet and spread my arms as if I would be able to actually catch it. Why? I am not sure.

The hog barely slowed down when it hit me. I grabbed for something to hold on to but before I knew it, I was being dragged along the roadway. It was then that I realized that I had a hold of one of the hog's large ears. I lost my grip and rolled with a dizzying spin into the tall grasses. By the time I was able to sit up, Hoss and the hog were near the main road. I tried to stand to my feet but I fell back onto the grass, totally out of breath and dizzy from the crash with the hog.

I heard Cliff's truck brakes squeal as he tried to stop the truck. I sat up and saw Cliff swerve to miss the hog and almost hit a tree.

He stepped out of the truck and shouted, "WHAT THE HELL IS GOING ON, BOY?" Both of his hands were in the air as he shouted.

I stood and tried to run toward him but felt dizzy from my unexpected ride.

When we met, I dropped onto my knees out of breath. "There are ... only two hogs left to find. I'll ... run after this one ... and keep my eye on it ... and you ... the other one is behind your house."

"The hogs are where and you want to do what?" asked Cliff as he helped me to my feet.

A moment later, Cliff started for the house as I ran out to the main road. When I arrived on the main road, I could see the hog and Hoss in the distance.

"HOSS, HOSS," I shouted, hoping he would return to me but he was too far down the road to hear me. However moments later, he stopped, turned and looked at me. I waved my arms and called to him again, and he trotted slowly back towards me. He seemed quite pleased that he had been on the job and was sure that we would be pleased with him.

Hoss and I followed the hog for about five minutes when off in the distance, I could hear Cliff beeping the horn of the truck. I turned to see him coming toward us, so I waited for him. When he stopped, he leaned out the window and said, "The other hog is in the pen. What the hell happened?"

I told him about the moose and what happened when it ran into the yard. He didn't seem angry, but tightened his lips and pulled his hat down closer to his eyebrows.

"Well, let's see if we can get this hog back to the yard," he said as he opened the door to let Hoss and I climb into the truck.

With all of the frantic panting and drooling, Hoss managed to get both of us wet but that seemed to be the least of our concern,

We drove down the road to where the hog was standing, out of breath and unable to go any farther. Stepping out of the truck, Cliff said, "Keep Hoss in the truck. If he gets out, the fool will chase the hog to town."

When I closed the door of the truck, Cliff waved his hand and said, "You go over there. Maybe we can chase this hog back to the yard. Go easy. I don't want to frighten it more then it is already."

An hour later, we had the last hog in the pen. Both of us walked over to the porch of the house and slumped into several old stuffed chairs.

"Sorry for scaring the moose but I didn't know that it would jump into the hog pen," I said in an apologetic tone as I hung my head and closed my eyes.

Cliff said nothing but went into the house and brought me an Orange Crush and a beer for himself.

"I'm sorry Cliff."

"No harm done," he said as he reached for a match to light his pipe. "Dogs will be dogs, hogs will be hogs and moose will be moose. By the way, how many hogs did you herd back to the yard?"

"I brought three back into the yard and there were two in the pen, but I don't know how many escaped."

"Three and two make five. Hmmmmm: that's strange. I only had four hogs in the first place and now you say that I have five?" Cliff taped the tobacco into his pipe with a wooden match and he tightened his lips.

I finished the bottle of Orange Crush as Cliff reached for his bottle of beer. "Yah know it sounds as if I have an extra hog."

"Cliff! Is it possible that one of the hogs from that truck accident we heard about found its way here? Remember about a week ago, a truck loaded with hogs rolled into the ditch? Maybe the extra hog is from that accident."

"Five miles is a long way through the bush, especially for a hog," he said as he puffed on his pipe. "But I guess it's possible." He began to stir the ashes in his pipe. After relighting it, smoke flowed from his mouth as he reached for his bottle of beer. "Suppose it's possible."

"Maybe it was at the back of the yard and came along with the ones I brought back into the yard," I said, optimistically, confident that I had solved the puzzle.

"Yah, I suppose it's possible," he said as he held the pipe in his hand and finished drinking his beer.

"Looks as if you have a free hog," I said, proud of the fact that he had more than what he had originally. Perhaps that news would make up for the kind of day we had just had.

Cliff disappeared into the house and returned with another Orange Crush and another bottle of beer. "I suppose," he said after he drank from the bottle. "But the fella that originally lost that hog in the accident would likely want it back. Out here, honesty is pretty important."

"But Cliff, here is your … I mean you have an extra hog. Think about it."

Smoke curled from his lips as he spoke. "If it was your hog and you knew that I had it, what would you say?"

Stunned by his question I scratched my head before speaking. "Dunno," I muttered, saddened by the possibility that we had to return what we had found and captured.

"Yes you do. You'd want it back," he said.

"Yah, I guess, so but how would he know?" I was disappointed by Cliff's loss.

"He doesn't need to know 'cause the important thing is that you and I know," continued Cliff.

We sat in silence: he puffing on his pipe and I sipping on my pop.

"Well, tomorrow we'll see if we can find the owner. By the way, you're all dirty. That hog sure took you for a ride … kinda reminded me of your last rodeo ride where the steer … er bull won."

"Hogs are tough to catch," I said as I dusted off my pants and tried to wipe away the grass stains on my arms.

"Here's a piece of advice. Don't stand in front of a run-a-way hog. Hogs don't like being herded. They're not like cows. You have to move slowly and make them think they're in control." He took another long drink from the bottle and placed the on the table, "Oh by the way, go and take Donut's saddle off. We'll load him into the truck and then I'll drive you back to Mabel's ranch. All of this hog chasing has made me hungry. How about you?"

When we arrived at Aunt Mabel's place, she had supper ready, so both of us washed our hands and sat at our usual places. She didn't ask why Donut and I had arrived with Cliff, so I said nothing and neither did Cliff but, when she asked why I was so dirty and scratched up, I walked to the water cooler for a drink as Cliff began to tell her about his trip to town.

When I returned to the round table, Cliff turned and tossed his hat onto a stuffed chair. "Say, I forgot to tell you about what I bought for you today. With all the excitement, I left it behind the seat of my truck."

I rushed out to Cliff's truck and moved the seat forward and opened the bag, and there to my surprise was a new cowboy hat. It was a bit too big but it was better than wearing my New York Yankees baseball cap.

When I opened the screen door and walked in, Cliff looked over and smiled. "You'd better not lose this one."

I pulled my chair up to the table and adjusted my new hat.

"No hats at the table please," she said as she closed the oven door.

I tossed my hat onto the stuffed chair where Cliff's hat was as she brought a large cooking pot to the table. When she removed the lid, both Cliff and I started laughing.

"What's wrong with the two of you? You've always liked roast pork before. So what's the problem?" she asked.

I don't remember seeing Cliff laugh so hard before or after.

CHAPTER 15

THE STUBBORN OLD BARN

One day while Cliff and I were in town, a short man with a scraggly beard came over to the truck. Most of the conversation between Cliff and the man was of no interest to me, so I just sat under a large poplar tree and enjoyed the shade because it was a hot day.

I watched trucks drive up and down the street, and several stopped in front of the post office. A dog trotted out into the dusty street and several people blew their horns at him, but he just ignored them. At front of the hardware store, three men sat on an old wooden bench, laughing and smoking crooked 'roll your own' cigarettes. At the end of the block, a man and his wife were painting a fence and behind their house someone was hoeing a garden. It was a very quiet day.

Cliff started the truck as I closed the door of the truck. He told me that on Thursday, we would be going to Trigve Gunderson's farm to help him tear down an old barn.

"Why not just burn it to the ground?" I remember asking.

"Well," replied Cliff and he shifted into second gear, "If you burn it down there are several problems. First, you'll have many nails in the soil and that isn't good for animals or tires. Secondly, the fire may spread and we wouldn't want that to happen."

"How big is the barn?"

"It's a very large one, so it could take a couple of days to finish the job. It's in such rough condition that a wind could bring it down at any time. I'm not sure if tearing it down is the way to get rid of it but that is what Trigve wants."

We drove home without much conversation. Cliff seemed to be in some deep thought about some other things, so I said nothing. After supper the three of us sat on the porch and enjoyed the evening rain showers and distant lightning.

The next morning, Cliff arrived very early and only beeped the horn of the truck. I closed the door of the house quietly so as not to disturb Aunt Mabel, and then I ran out to meet him.

"Mabel still in bed?" he asked as he backed the truck up before shifting into first gear.

"Yah, she set some food out for me last night before she went to bed."

"How did you manage to wake up in time?"

"She set the alarm for me. Boy is that thing a noisy clock. It's the one with large bells on the top. It kept me awake, although I am getting used to the large clock at the end of the hall 'cause it chimes every half hour."

"Yah, I have one of those alarm clocks myself and have hated it since the day I bought it, but it does work."

About an hour later, we drove into a farmyard where I could see six other trucks parked near the corral. Men were walking around a very large old barn that had huge holes in the roof. It looked as if the barn had never been painted. A flock of pigeons flew in and out of the openings in the roof. Cliff was right. It looked as if it would collapse in the first windstorm.

"How old is it?" I asked as I stepped from the truck.

"Nobody knows. It's been here before Trigve bought the place, so we really don't know," said Cliff.

As we approached the group of men, one said, "Trig, there's nothin' here worth savin'. 'Sides it's a bit dangerous for us to crawl onto the roof or go inside and start tearin' off boards. The wood's dried out and not worth usin' for anything else except firewood in winter."

A second man pushed back his hat as he looked inside the barn. "There are two main support poles holding up the roof. Why don't we pull them out and let it collapse. That will make it easier and safer to tear apart once it is on the ground."

"Yah, it would be safer to tear it apart when it's down on the ground than while it's standing," agreed Cliff.

Trigve stepped into the barn and walked over to one of the large support poles. "Der stronger dan vhat you guys tink. If you really tink it vould vork den," he paused to scratch his chin, "I guess dat is vhat we vill do."

"How many tractors do you have, Trig," asked Cliff.

"Yust two Yohn Deeres, but dey isn't so big, you know," he replied.

"Well, let's get them here." Cliff said, "Harold, can you see if you can find chains and Waldo, can you tear the rear door off the barn by the time we get back?"

"What do you want me to do?" asked a man with a large red nose and thick glasses.

"You go with Waldo. He'll need some help."

Fifteen minutes passed before the two faded green and yellow tractors arrived at the barn. One of the tractors was like my Uncle's tractor, an AR model, and the other was so old that the lettering on the side of it was too faded for me to read. Both puffed and vibrated as they awaited the task before them. The men carried chains and cables into the barn and after digging at the base of each support pole, they wrapped a chain around it and carried the other end out to the waiting tractors. It looked rather simple. All the tractors had to do was to pull the base of two poles out and the barn would collapse, causing the roof to fall.

"Vhat if dis don't vork?" asked Trigve.

"Trust us Trig," said the man with the red nose and thick glasses, "This old barn will come down."

I looked up as the flock of pigeons continued to circle overhead. I wondered if they knew that their home was about to be destroyed.

Cliff climbed onto the AR model and pushed the hand clutch. It puffed and started to move forward. He drove to the front of the barn and then backed up so that the chain could be hooked up to it. In the meantime, a tall man drove the other John Deere to the rear of the barn and backed it up to the barn door so that the chain and cable could be hooked up to it.

All of the men walked into the barn to review their plan.

"The tractor at the front of the barn should start the pull first because it is stronger and once the pole has started to move, then it will be time to let the tractor at the rear of the barn begin to pull," said a short chubby man.

Cliff sped up the engine. It puffed and vibrated as he slowly moved the hand clutch until the chain was tight. At the same time, the man at the rear of the barn sped up the engine and moved the clutch until the chain was tight. Once both chains were tight, Trigve motioned to them to start pulling.

Overhead the flock of pigeons circled, looking for a place to land.

Both tractors puffed and snorted as if they were in a pulling contest. When Trigve lowered his hands, Cliff and the other man pushed the hand clutches of the tractors, and both tractors began to pull. At that moment, Cliff's tractor's front wheels came off the ground and it seemed as if it would flip over backwards while the tractor at the rear seemed to suddenly be moving forward. All of a sudden, one of the support beams fell with a large crash but the old barn did not collapse. It leaned more to the west than ever before.

"Vell, dats one of doz poles. Vhat do ve do now?" asked Trigve, when the men gathered again to review and discuss their plan.

I spotted two cats running out of the barn. Fortunately for them, the barn didn't come down while they were inside. They disappeared into the long grass with Trigve's brown hound right behind them.

"Now vhat?" asked Trigve as he removed his tattered red cap.

After some discussion, the group decided to use both tractors at the front of the barn, and so they hooked up both tractors to the last support pole. The engines were revved up and both began to pull.

Again, both tractors had their front wheels bouncing dangerously off the ground.

"**SHUT IT DOWN**!" shouted Cliff. "This is too dangerous."

Circling overhead, I watched the flock of pigeons as they landed on the roof. To me they seemed nervous as they looked down at the men and tractors.

For the next half hour, the work crew discussed what they would do to bring the old barn down. No one seemed to agree as they walked around the barn several times. They continued arguing what would work and what would not work.

Finally, all of the men went to the farmhouse and drank some coffee that the lady of the house had brewed. By the smell of it, I could tell that it was something that was far too strong for me to drink.

"Voot you like a glass of milk, yah?" asked the tall lady in the colorful apron.

I shook my head and replied, "No thanks. I'll be OK."

"Vell, how about some a der fruit? Vhat about da apples? Do you eat apples?"

I managed to eat two apples as the men discussed the challenge before them.

"Trig," said Cliff, "You used to have some dynamite that you used for blowing up beaver dams. Do you still have some?"

"Yawh, but I tink it is too oldt and may not have much poof left, anymore."

The man with the red nose smiled and started to chuckle. "By gum, who cares if it's old? If yah have to, just double the amount."

"Are you two crazy? A blast of dynamite will bring the barn down alright, but it'll spread the wood all over the place," said a man with a white hat.

"We'll just dig around the support pole a little more and put the dynamite at the base. That will loosen it and then we can pull it down," said Cliff.

When the crew reentered the barn, they began to dig around the last support pole. When they had dug down about two feet, dynamite was placed at the base of the pole. Trigve laid several sticks of dynamite and then called "**DARES DAH FIRE IN DARE HOLE**!" and all of the men ran to clear the area.

I remember seeing the flame of a match near the hole when suddenly Trigve stood to his feet and started to run for the front door. Just before reaching the door, his foot caught on the cables and chains that had been used earlier when they tried to pull the barn down. He tried to stand to his feet but fell against the inner wall. In a moment, Cliff darted in the front door, grabbed Trigve's arm and pulled him to safety. They ran as fast as they could and to dove under one of the tractors. A moment later, there was a tremendous;

BOOOOMMM!

Dust puffed from every corner and crack of the barn, almost as if the old barn was breathing. The pigeons flapped their way through a hole in the roof a moment after the blast and one of them dropped to the ground. A cat ran over to grab it and carried it off into the long grass.

Cliff and Trigve lay on the ground, glad to be far enough away from harm or so they thought. The shingles slivered into millions of pieces and the weather vane dropped to the ground near them. Cliff stood to his feet, grabbed Trigve by the arm and dragged him behind an old hay wagon.

When the dust settled, the old barn was still standing but now it had a large hole in the roof. A gray and white cat scurried out of the barn and as it ran it shook its head from side to side.

"Say Trigve, I'll bet you five dollars that if you check on that gray and white cat, you'll find that he's deaf," said the man with the white hat as he leaned against the tractor and laughed. Soon all of them were laughing.

Cautiously, the men approached the barn, unsure of what would happen next or what they should be doing with the old barn. Both tractors were covered in dust and pieces of wood. Fortunately there was no damage to either of them.

As the flock of pigeons circled the barn, Trigve stood to his feet. "Now vhat should ve do?" he asked the men who were dusting off their hats and shoulders. "How vill ve git da cables and de chains back in der? Who vill go in der now?"

Cliff and the fellow with the white hat inched their way into the front of the barn to see what damage had resulted from the blast. The rest of the men remained at a safe distance.

"The center support pole is missing and there is only a little piece holding this building up," the voice of the man in the white hat echoed in the empty barn.

"You'd better get out before it comes down," called the man with the red nose.

"There's nothing to hook the chains and cables onto. The entire center of the barn is missing. I'm not sure what's holding it up," said the man with the white hat.

I watched as the two men stepped away from the barn and at the same moment I noticed a flock of pigeons land on the roof. As soon as they landed on the roof, the old barn creaked loudly and slowly crumbled to the ground.

Cliff and the man with the white hat heard the creaking and suddenly bolted for cover. As the barn finally settled the hayloft door fell open. The barn was in its final resting place. The flock of pigeons flew away and a yellow cat stepped out of a hole in the roof and ran off into the long grasses.

"We should have let the pigeons bring it down from the beginning. They did a good job. Don't you think?" I asked as I rushed over to Cliff.

"Well, the barn's down. Do you want us to help you clean up?" asked Cliff. "I sure hope there aren't any more cats hiding in there."

We left about an hour after supper. As we drove home, I turned to Cliff, "Say, Cliff, did he use too much dynamite?"

"He should have used more. Then we wouldn't have had to tear so many boards apart," he said as he winked at me.

Cliff laughed as he shifted into high gear. "If it hadn't been for those pigeons landing on the roof, who knows how many sticks of dynamite we would have needed to bring it down. 'Sides those cats were lucky. I wonder how many of their lives they lost today when the blast went off, especially that yellow one."

"Well that's one way to get rid of a barn and a dozen cats," I said as I tipped my hat back. After all, tearing down an old barn is hard work.

CHAPTER 16

PADDLE OAR ELSE

When Cliff invited me along on a canoeing trip with several of his friends, I was sure that my life couldn't get any better. He told me of the many annual trips he had taken on the Ram River in the Yahatinda area of the Rocky Mountains.

Not sure what a Yahatinda was, I repeated the word "Yaha … what?"

"It's a very large area with several rivers and large valleys. The Red Deer River flows through that whole area and eventually passes through town of Red Deer. Then it makes it way through the Badlands of Drumheller, where all the dinosaurs were.

"Where does it go from there?" I asked, eager to hear more.

"I think it joins the South Saskatchewan River and then they become one."

"That must be a large river by then," Aunt Mabel interjected.

"I know about those rivers. They join together at a very small town called Estuary, before it flows on to the Hudson's Bay and the Atlantic Ocean," I interrupted, proud that I knew some geography.

"How did you know that?" asked Aunt Mabel.

I studied that in Mr. Alergoth's class, 'sides my uncle lives in Leader, Saskatchewan near the town of Estuary and he took my father and me fishing where those rivers join."

"Well, that's one place that I've never been to," said Cliff as he puffed on his pipe.

"My Uncle Bill took us in a boat onto the river and we anchored right where the two rivers meet. One was very muddy and the other quite clear. We didn't catch any fish, but it was neat to see."

Aunt Mabel returned with more coffee for Cliff and as they talked, my mind wandered off to the possibilities of this trip. "I've never been in a canoe but remembered reading about the Coureur des Bois, who were early Canadian Fur Traders in eastern Canada."

"What?" asked Cliff.

"We'll be like the Coureur des Bois," I said, anxious to share my schooling with Cliff.

"Coureur de … who?" asked Cliff again. His eyes narrowed and he cocked his head to the side.

"My teacher, Mrs. Flynn told the class that 'Coureur des Bois' is French for Runners of the Woods. They were fur traders who sold furs to the Hudson's Bay Company. They trapped without the permission of the French authorities, and later were called voyageurs." I said, proud that I knew something that Cliff didn't.

"Where did you learn all that from?" asked Cliff as he shook the ashes from his pipe.

"In Social Studies class."

Aunt Mabel smiled at me. "Did any of the explorers travel in that area?"

"Yeh. My teacher told us that a man, named David Thompson and his men traveled somewhere in this area but found some of the rivers difficult to travel on so they stayed for the winter, but the trip didn't turn out very well."

"That's why it is called the David Thompson area," said Cliff as he puffed on his pipe. He sounded rather amused and surprised.

"That's my nephew," said Aunt Mabel proudly as she ruffled my hair and then folded her arms across her chest.

"Was David Thompson a Cour whats it?" continued Cliff.

"No they were in eastern Canada and the United States. This David Thompson and his men were explorers and map makers," I continued.

Cliff stirred his coffee and smiled at me. "That's good, I never knew much about the French down east."

"Do you like history," asked Aunt Mabel.

"It is one of my favorite subjects. So when do we go canoeing?" I asked, eager to get started.

"Sunday morning."

For the next few days, I worked as hard as I could. I made sure that the garden was hoed, that some hay was gathered by the slough and the fence near the entry to the ranch. At nights, I would lie awake, guessing what it would be like to be in a canoe on a river where explorers had been.

Sunday morning finally arrived. It was early when Cliff came to the ranch for his coffee with Aunt Mabel. When he had drunk several cups of coffee, he packed the truck with food that Aunt Mabel had prepared, and finally we were on our way. Aunt Mabel waved good bye as we drove out of the yard.

For two hours, I asked questions about the river and where we would camp. Fortunately, Cliff was a patient man and answered all of my questions. At one point I asked about what it was like to ride in a canoe and he told me "Don't try to stand up in the canoe whatever you do, and when I tell you to paddle, you paddle on the side of the canoe that I tell you to. Other than that, the river does most of the work. Our job is to keep the canoe upright and away from the rocks. We don't want to damage the canoe on the rocks."

"But we don't have a canoe. Where will we find one," I asked.

"My friends are bringing an extra one, so don't worry."

When we arrived at a fork in the road, we turned down a road that was very sandy and crooked. The trees smacked the windshield as we bounced along and when we rounded a corner, I spotted another truck with two canoes, parked ahead of us. When we stopped beside them, Cliff introduced me to the two men that were waiting there. As they spoke to each other, I walked over to see the canoes and canvass packages on the back of their trucks. I was amazed at the tents, grub and necessary gear for this trip.

Eager to get started, I walked over to the edge of the ditch and down to a small, sandy knoll to look off into the distance. I remembered my fishing experience with the bear and laughed at myself for having been so stupid.

When Cliff called, I ran to help him unload the canoe from the truck. After working hard and groaning loudly, we finally had the canoes off the trucks. For about half-an-hour, we carried the canoes inch by inch along a rough trail and at times I was sure that we would never get to the river. We stopped several times because of the trees that had fallen across the path. At one place, I stumbled over a sharp rock that was on the edge of the trail, and I almost fell. My back ached and it reminded me of my last rodeo ride.

I was exhausted when we finally arrived at the stream and wanted to lie down, but Cliff reminded me that we needed to go back to bring all of the grub, tents and camping equipment that we brought for the trip. I just wanted to lie down and die somewhere by the bushes.

It took about an hour to carry all of the food, paddles, tent and camping equipment to where we had left the canoes. I was so tired that I lay on the grass for a rest. Soon Cliff called to me and insisted that we keep working.

John and Paul had their canoe ready before we did, so they sat on the shore and waited until Cliff and I were packed and ready to go. Just before leaving, Cliff passed a brown bottle around and the men took several large swallows from it and handed the bottle back to Cliff. The men talked a little longer and then, Cliff said, "OK, gents let's roll."

Cliff climbed into the canoe and moved to the far end and then told me to push the canoe off the sand bar so it would go in the water. I pushed, but I couldn't budge it. Finally, John came to help me, and soon Cliff and I were floating down the river. Eventually, the others got into their canoe and managed to follow us.

It was an unusual feeling to float in a canoe but I learned very quickly that making a sudden move could be disastrous. In fact, any slight move made it feel as if we were going to tip over.

"Just sit still and let it carry you. Let your body relax and be part of the canoe, and whatever you do, don't make any sudden moves," instructed Cliff.

At first, I was stiff and unable to paddle because I was afraid the canoe would tip over. It seemed to wobble so much that I often grabbed the side of the canoe to hang on. It took me some time to finally understand how to paddle. Cliff was patient with me as I tried to follow his instructions. He maneuvered around rocks until we finally came to a long narrow part of the river. The water was higher than I expected and certainly flowed faster than I could have guessed.

I gripped the paddle tightly and paddled, even though my arms were hurting. Cliff encouraged me to keep paddling until we finally reached calmer water. I relaxed and looked around and was amazed to see elk, moose and even some mountain sheep in the distance. They watched as we silently floated by them. I lost count of how many animals we actually saw. If it were not for the bubbling water and Cliff orders, it would have been very quiet.

I heard a noise in the distance and turned to look back at Cliff as he pointed to the right and yelled, "PADDLE HARD FOR THAT CLEARING!"

I didn't have the heart to tell him that I was too tired, so I closed my eyes and paddled until my muscles burned. We bobbed like corks on the river and there were several times when I was sure we would capsize. The water around us was bubbling and splashing into the canoe and I suddenly realized that we were in danger.

"HOW COME THE RIVER IS SO ROUGH?" I shouted.

"KEEP PADDLING. THESE ARE RAPIDS. DON'T QUIT, YAH HEAR? PADDLE AS IF YOUR LIFE DEPENDS ON IT."

My arms hurt and I was sure that I could not go any further, when suddenly the river became smooth again. Hour after hour we flowed with the current as the other canoe followed at a considerable distance. Several hours after our departure, Cliff pointed to a clearing in the distance and said, "PADDLE FOR THAT CLEARING AND WE'LL STOP FOR A REST."

Those were the best sounding words I had heard in a long time. When all of us arrived at the clearing, I rested as the men leaned against logs and sipped on Cliff's brown bottle. John and Cliff smoked their pipes and eventually Paul and I fell asleep.

After they had emptied Cliff's brown bottle, we were back on the water. We had covered quite a distance before Cliff called for me to head toward a stack of logs. I was glad for the break until I found out that we would have to carry our supplies and the canoe over a ledge so we could avoid a waterfall. That was more work than I could ever imagine. This took about two hours and I was so tired that I had to lie on the ground to catch my breath.

"In early spring this is a dangerous area. Sometimes there is so much water flowing through here that it is impossible to use this river for several weeks." said Cliff.

Late in the afternoon, we made camp by some very tall trees. The canoes were dragged on shore and overturned, and soon the tents were up.

John agreed to cook and the food was very good. It tasted a bit different than what I expected, but when you're hungry, you can eat anything.

"Hey kid. Do you know what you're eatin'?" asked John as he lit his pipe.

"Don't know. What is it?"

"Well, that is the finest moose stew this side of the Rocky Mountains," Cliff said as he looked over to Paul who was rolling a cigarette.

"Moose stew?"

They all laughed as I poked at the food in my plate.

"Yes. It will stick to your ribs and give you strength for tomorrow."

I had never eaten moose stew before but it was good and I was so hungry. I tried not to think about moose meat.

"Say kid, do you know what is significant about that large tree over there?" asked Paul as he pointed to an extra tall tree in the distance.

"No."

"It's called a Lodge Pole. A Lodge Pole is a tall tree that is used as a marker to let hunters, hikers, surveyors and lumber companies know where they are and where they're going. Originally, they were used by explorers and surveyors to lay out maps," continued Cliff.

I never heard the rest of the explanation because my eyes were heavy and I guess I fell asleep. Cliff woke me and sent me into the tent and I was asleep again as soon as I lay my head down.

I suddenly awoke with a full bladder. It was still bright outside so I sat up in my sleeping bag and pulled on my cowboy boots. Outside, I was surprised to see the men sitting by the fire, smoking and telling jokes.

When I returned to my tent, I fell asleep again and didn't even hear Cliff when he arrived. My dreams were about overturning canoes and water rapids and water falls. During the night I woke up feeling cold, so I reached for a towel that lay near Cliff's jacket and used it to cover myself to keep warm. I dreamed of riding at the rodeo and about Alva.

I opened my eyes as Cliff called, "Come on Tex, it's time to get up."

After a breakfast of bacon, scrambled eggs and fried potatoes, we were in the canoes again but this time I found it even hard to paddle. My shoulders ached from yesterday's hard work and my ribs ached too. I paddled because I was too afraid to disappoint Cliff. At times, I kept my eyes closed trying to ignore the pain.

During dinner, I lay down to rest my aching body and when it was time to go, I could barely walk to the canoe.

"What's wrong with you, Tex?" asked Paul.

"I'm so sore that I can hardly move."

"I'll handle the rest of the day," said Cliff. "You relax 'cause the rest of the trip is pretty smooth. We'll just flow with the current."

The second evening was Cliff's turn to cook. He asked me to peel potatoes and gather more wood for the evening fire. Cliff's stew was very good and while the others sat around the fire and talked, I crawled into our tent and fell asleep.

During the night, I heard a noise; one like a frying pan falling onto a rock. In my sleep, I stretched and was about to roll over when I heard the noise again. I opened my eyes and lay perfectly still. Again I heard the noise and I cautiously opened the tent flap to see what it was, but all I could see was the glow of the dying fire. I rubbed my eyes and squinted for a moment and finally I could see an object moving where the pots and dishes were. I heard it again and then Cliff reached over and put his hand on my arm.

In the silence, I listened to my heart beat.

"It's probably a bear," Cliff whispered.

"A bear!" The rest of my sentence was muffled as Cliff held his hand over my mouth.

"Yeh. He's probably licking the frying pan. He couldn't find any food so he's going where he smells food."

"Where is the food?" I whispered.

"We put it up in a tree away from here."

"What if he finds it?"

"He'll have to climb the tree." As he whispered, I looked down and saw a rifle in his hands.

"Are you going to shoot him?" I whispered.

"No need to. I'll use it only if we're in danger."

The small glow of the dying fire reflected off the barrel of his rifle.

"I hope you can shoot as well as Aunt Mabel," I whispered.

"No one can shoot that good. Now shhhhssss," he whispered with his pointer finger pressed against my lips.

Eventually the bear left the campsite and Cliff fell asleep but this time I couldn't sleep because of his snoring.

The third day we traveled down a very narrow part of the river and sometime after lunch I was surprised to see a large bull moose standing in the middle of the river ahead of us. He had been drinking water but when we rounded the bend, he lifted his head to stare us.

"Don't fret. He's more curious than dangerous," comforted Cliff.

I was glad that we were the second canoe and not leading. John and Paul slowed their canoe as they neared him. The moose lowered his head and then sniffed the air. It was a sign to us to stay clear of him. Fortunately, he stepped onto the shore as they passed by. Then the moose began to paw the ground, just like the yearling bull had done. My heart started racing.

When they were almost beside him, I looked back at Cliff and saw that he had placed his rifle on his lap.

"Now what?" I asked, hoping that Cliff had a better plan.

"Just be quiet and don't paddle. Just wait, but when I tell you to paddle, you paddle like hell. Yah hear?"

I nodded my head and waited for his call. "If he charges us, what do I do? Remember that I'm in the front of the canoe."

"If he gets into the water and gets too close lean backwards and get into the water.

We neared the moose and it stepped back into the river with its front feet.

My eyes were riveted on it as my heart pounded so loudly that I could hear it in my ears. In a few moments, we would be beside him and about fifteen feet from him. I decided that if he came at us, I'd dive into the water and swim for the other shore.

As we passed, Cliff used his paddle to splash water at him. Spray flew up at his face and he stepped back as we passed by. **"PADDLE!"** Cliff yelled. **"PADDLE LIKE HELL!"**

I leaned into the paddle and we started to pick up speed and soon we were in the current and moving along quickly. Moments later, I could hear Cliff say, "OK. WE'RE OK. You can slow down."

My shoulders ached after that paddling crisis. They burned and I felt as if I needed to put them into the cold river water. The strong sun also made my skin burn and I was in pain and longing for a break. When it was time to camp for the night, I could barely wait until my feet were on ground again.

That evening, my chore was to collect firewood. During my forage, I found a bush with large berries on it and soon was spending more time picking and eating berries than gathering firewood.

When I returned, almost everyone had finished eating. Cliff was smoking his pipe, while the others were playing cards. The food was tasty and when they asked what took so long, I told them about the bush with the large black berries.

I lay on the sand and looked up at the stars, and tried to remember what I had learned about them in science class. It was so quiet and nice to be away from the city. I decided that I would do whatever I could to live in the country when I was older. I thought about my brother Oswald and it was the first time in my life that I missed him. Even though he was six years younger than me, he was the best brother anyone could have.

The warm sand made me feel comfortable and the sound of bubbling water made me sleepy. I remembered watching a falling star but not much after that.

When I rolled over, I realized that I had fallen asleep on the riverbank, and the evening air had become quite cool. As I stood up, I shivered and pulled my jacket over my neck. Then I realized that all of the men had gone to bed and I was left out there alone. I moved toward the tents but was not sure which one was Cliff's. As I blinked my eyes and moved toward them to see more clearly, I stepped on a twig and it cracked loudly. I stopped instantly, too frightened to move.

It was too dark to tell which tent was ours. There was a moment when I thought that I had better stay outside for the night but the cool air had a way of making me choose a tent. When I heard snoring from all of the tents, I knew that this was going to be a difficult task.

"Cliff," I whispered loudly, if that were possible. "Cliff!"

The snoring stopped in the tent on the left.

"Cliff," I whispered again.

A flashlight shone its beam onto the inside of the tent flap and I knew it was Cliff's tent.

"Thanks," I managed to say as I knelt on my sleeping bag. "How did you know I wasn't a bear?" I asked.

"Well, there're two clues," he said as he turned off his flashlight. "First, bears don't whisper and secondly, none of them know my name."

I put my face into my jacket that was my pillow and laughed. By the time I had zipped up my sleeping bag, I heard him snoring again. Somehow I managed to fall asleep.

CHAPTER 17

MANNY'S REVENGE

With only one week left before my return to city life, I decided to do whatever it took to enjoy myself. Selfishly, I ate more cookies, drank more soda pop, rode Donut more often and spent less time on the porch with Cliff and Aunt Mabel. Horseback rides in the quiet forests became more frequent and valuable. Often, when I returned, Aunt Mabel would subtly remind me that she was worried about my safety but I assured her that I would be all right.

On one of our trips to town to pick up the mail, Aunt Mabel became ill and she asked me to drive her home. Though surprised by her request, I was up to the task and carefully maneuvered the Fargo over the ten miles back to the Broken Antler Ranch. I didn't drive very fast and often looked at her as she slept, and wondered why she didn't want to go back to the hospital.

One day, I realized that she might need wood for the winter, so I spent the rest of the day gathering, chopping and stacking wood for her. I knew that it would not be enough but I tried to convince myself that I would do more when I had time and energy.

After a small lunch on the porch, I loaded several bales of hay that were near the slough and brought them to the barn with the Fargo. While I worked I wished I was stronger and able to do more because she was alone. I made several trips but soon ran out of energy.

"Of all my nephews who have been with me, you have been the most helpful," she said as she sipped from her cup and then ruffled my hair. "One day, you'll look back at this summer and remember how nice it was to be away from the city."

"Well, this has been the best summer I've ever had. I miss my brother and wish that he could be here."

She smiled at me as I continued, "Maybe he'll be the next nephew to come here for summer vacation but there are some things that I need to attend to first," she said after she emptied the cup.

Both of us could see Cliff's truck coming over the hill. When he was only a few minutes from the yard, I looked at her. "Cliff is such a nice guy. You should marry him," I hinted in a soft tone so as not to upset her.

She smiled and then waved at him.

"Howdy to you," he said as he stepped from his truck. When he arrived on the porch, he reached over and pulled my hat over my eyes and said, "Well, I hear that you're about to go home."

"Yeah," I said disappointedly.

He lit his pipe as Aunt Mabel went into the house. When she returned, she brought a cup of coffee for him.

"So, what's exciting in your world?" she asked him in a teasing way.

"Well, tonight there's going to a party for Manny Cunningham at Tom and Freda's. He's turnin' forty tomorrow. They invited us to a party for him tonight. It would be nice to go. What do you think? Do you feel up to it?"

"Forty, is that all he is? He looks older than that," said Aunt Mabel as she stirred her coffee.

"We've been invited to come. Are you up to going?" he asked again.

"Always ready for a party, I guess," she said as she closed the buttons of her sweater.

"It starts at seven and there'll be a dance and I hear Dunya Kline is coming, so there will be lots of good Ukrainian food. I love those perogies and vereniki. Mind you, she's not as good a cook as you, Mabel."

"I'm glad you clarified that. Actually, she is a much better cook than I am but thank you for the compliment. I needed that, especially today," she said as Cliff went into the house.

When he returned to the porch with the pot of coffee he asked, "Well, do you think you can go?"

"Sounds good to me. It's been the best invitation I've had in a long time," she said. "I'll have to wear my new dress. It's the one with the white collar and small bow at the waist."

"And wear that new scarf of yours. It looks so good on you," said Cliff as he reached for his pipe and pouch of tobacco.

"Will I be able to go?" I asked, hoping that they would not leave me behind.

"Sure thing. Before we go, I want to go to Manny's place and pull some tricks on him. He'll be at the auction sale in the town of Caroline this afternoon, so I know he'll go directly to the Tom and Freda's before going home. That'll give us plenty of time."

"Us?" she asked as she placed her empty cup on the handrail of the veranda.

"Us, the three of us."

"The two of you can go because the phrase, 'plenty of time' worries me, besides I'll be at your place at six so we can travel together. I don't want to know what tricks you're going to pull on him. That way I will be legitimately surprised when I hear of what has happened to him."

"Sounds good to me," Cliff said as he finished the coffee. "I'm ready, so let's go," he said as he looked at me and grabbed his hat.

Cliff and I drove to the Cunningham farm and on the way there, he told me of all the things he planned to do. A half hour later, we turned into Manny's yard. It was a messy farmyard. Chickens roamed freely and so did the hogs. Weeds were waist high at the front door of his house and none of the buildings had paint on them.

"Manny's a bachelor. How can you tell that he needs a wife? She'd get him to do some work around here," said Cliff as he stepped from the truck and closed the door. He carefully looked around and the only thing that we could see moving in the yard was an old three-legged dog that limped over to us.

"What's his name?"

"Lucky, 'cause he's lucky to be alive," responded Cliff.

"That's kind of dumb. What happened?"

"I don't remember. Well, let's get busy."

"What do we do first?" I asked, eager to get involved.

"You bring the hammer that's behind the seat and some of those three inch nails and oh, bring that can of red paint and the brush.

Moments later, Cliff was nailing the front door of Manny's

house shut. "There, that will cause him some concern. After all, he pulled some tricks on me when I turned forty."

Moments later Cliff carried a can of red paint over to Manny's green John Deere tractor and painted the faded green, metal seat bright red. "There, he can't miss that," he said with a chuckle.

We spent the next half hour chasing several hogs into the small building at the far end of the yard. When we entered it, we had to take some time to calm the hogs but when Cliff was able to get near them, he painted the number 40 on the side of each hog. The numbers were very large and easy to see because they were painted with bright red paint.

"Let's just hope they don't roll in the mud until Manny gets home," said Cliff as he carried the red paint can and brush back to his truck.

We caught several cows and tied them to the windmill and pulled the empty hay wagon into the middle of the yard. We found a pair of underwear on the clothesline and decided to tie them on the top of the windmill.

"Before we go, I want to paint the outhouse seat red," he said. When he returned he chuckled, "That should do it."

When we were about to leave, Cliff closed the lid of the paint can and placed it behind the seat. Then he reached into the back of his truck and took an old rag and wiped his hands on it, wrapped the paint brush into it and tossed it into the back of his truck.

"Let's go to the party," he said as he started the truck. When we had driven down the road some distance, Cliff stopped the truck and tossed the rag, with the paint brush into the long grass in the ditch.

"There that will take care of the evidence," he said as he revved the engine and spun the tires.

"What about the can of paint?" I asked.

"I'll drop it off at my ranch when we meet Mabel. I need that can of paint to paint the rest of the barn."

When we arrived at his ranch, Aunt Mabel was waiting for us in Cliff's house.

"I don't want to know what you all did, in case he asks me," she said as she brushed her hair in front of the mirror next to the front door. "By the way, Cliff, you'd better change your pants 'cause there's red paint on your thigh and if Manny sees that, well … you know who'll get the blame for whatever you did."

After Cliff changed, we drove to Tom and Freda's farm and when we arrived there were eight other trucks parked in the yard. A small collie came out to greet us and it escorted us into the yard as it barked and ran beside Cliff's truck.

"You'll like it here," said Cliff. "Eddy and Bernice are nice kids. They're about your age. I'll introduce them to you, so you don't have to spend the entire evening listening to us old folks."

Aunt Mabel carried a round chocolate cake into the house as Cliff and I walked over to the corral, where we saw the kids playing.

"Hey, Eddy," Cliff called. "I'd like you to meet a friend of mine. He's from the city but don't let that make you think he's strange. He can ride; in fact he won the Calf Riding contest in Rocky Mountain House, back in the beginning of July."

Eddy started to walk toward me and as he did, he tipped his cowboy hat.

"That's Bernice, over there." Cliff whispered. "Kinda nice, don't you think?"

She was younger than me and from what I could see she looked better than any of the girls in my school. I smiled at her and instantly my cheeks felt warm.

Eddy and I shook hands as Cliff turned and started for the house.

"Have fun," he shouted over his shoulder. Eddy's a decent kid. You'll like him."

"So, what do you want to do?" asked Eddy as he leaned against a fence post.

"Don't know. What are the choices?"

"Well, let's eat first and then we'll go for a horseback ride. I'll show you the lake. We have a boat out there. Come on," he said as he started for the house.

Manny Cunningham was surprised. He kept saying, "If I knew that you would have done this for me, I'd have had my fortieth birthday sooner, if not more often."

I looked around the room at the nice people and smiled as Aunt Mabel introduced me to them.

Then all of us circled the table and grabbed whatever sandwiches we could carry. It didn't matter where I stood or went, Bernice was always somewhere in front of me. She always smiled and I began to feel embarrassed. When she was not in the room, I found myself looking for her. She made me feel warm inside and kind of weird. I secretly hoped that she didn't lisp.

After we could eat no more, Eddy and I walked to the barn.

"You can ride Bernie's horse, 'cause she'll stay home to help mom with the dishes. That's girls' work you know, so us men can do other things. Right?"

"Yah, I guess so," I said. "Will she mind?"

"Naw," he said as he opened the corral gate and walked toward the barn.

About twenty minutes later, both horses were saddled and we were riding toward a small lake. Bernice's horse was much bigger than Donut and reacted quicker to my reins, so I had to learn how to ride differently. Twice I almost fell off when the horse turned suddenly. Before I knew it, I was riding with my hand on the saddle horn again. I tried not to let Eddie see, so I rode behind him.

"Whaaaatts theeee horrrsse's naaaaame?" I stammered at the horse trotted.

"Butterfly."

We talked about all kinds of things. He was in the same grade at school as I, and enjoyed arithmetic, as I did. He had never read a Hardy Boys book but read other books like Tom Sawyer.

When we neared the lake, Eddy slowed his horse, dismounted and tied it to a tree near a rickety pier. I watched as he ran toward the boat.

"Come on," he yelled, so I tied Bernice's horse and walked down the crooked pier.

"Are there any fish in this lake?" I asked.

"No, just minnows, but if you want, we can row across to the other side."

We rowed around the lake and before we knew it, the moon was starting to rise in the east. It made a very nice reflection on the lake and I could hear loons calling as ducks and Canada geese flew overhead. By the time we returned to the pier, it was very dark and I had to feel my way over to Bernice's horse.

"Do these horses know the way home," I asked nervously.

"Sure do," said Eddy as he climbed into the saddle. "Do you want to race?"

"Naw! A quiet ride will be just fine," I said, but by then he shouted, "Come on Barney, let's go." He snapped the reins on the horse's rump and I heard galloping in the darkness and knew I was alone.

I had just turned Bernice's horse to put my boot into the stirrup when something large flew past me. Its flapping wings made the horse jump. I grabbed for the saddle horn but before I could grip the reins, Butterfly started to gallop. Fortunately I was able to pull myself into the saddle and suddenly I was off to the ride of my life. There were moments when I wished I could be on the back of a steer at the rodeo instead of this crazy horse that was racing across a field I did not know. The darkness was blinding so I had no idea where we were going. "Please God let this horse see where it is going. I don't want to die." Suddenly we went under some trees and then Butterfly jumped a log. That is when I closed my eyes.

Suddenly I realized that we had passed Eddy. I heard him yelling at his horse but I was too scared to look over my shoulder to see where he was. As we galloped along, my hat flew off. I wondered what Aunt Mabel would say when she found out that I lost another hat.

The moon appeared when several clouds passed by and I could see some buildings and haystacks to my left. Bernice's horse never lost stride but ran as if it were scared as I was. Its mane struck my face when I rounded the corner of the haystacks. I could see the lights of the house in the distance and I feared that we wouldn't be able to stop.

Moments later, we raced into the corral and the horse stopped suddenly by the water trough. In fact, it stopped so suddenly that I flipped over its head and landed on the ground with a large thud. The horse stepped sideways and almost stepped on me and a few seconds later, Eddy stopped beside me.

"Say, that was quite a ride. I never knew that Butterfly could run that fast," he gasped. "Cliff was right; you can ride. I've never lost a race before. We should try this again."

Gasping for my breath, I staggered to my feet as I grabbed the reins of the horse before it could wander off. I was breathing heavily and was somewhat dizzy.

"Noooo, I don't want to ride any more 'cause I ate too much." At that moment, my stomach was so upset that I was sure that I'd throw up, so I turned the horse so Eddie couldn't see me.

"You OK?" he asked. "It looked like you fell off. Are you OK?"

"Just not used to this horse," I wheezed. "It does run well," I said in a confident tone, "but it's a lousy stopper and I ate too much."

"Yah, I know. Bernie has complained about that to dad before, but it was a cheap horse."

After we had removed the saddles and brushed the horses, we started for the house. I was glad that it was dark so that he could not see me limping from my fall.

About fifty feet from the house we could hear a banjo and a piano playing. As we stepped into the room, I could see Cliff and Mrs. Cunningham dancing as if they were my age. I looked for Aunt Mabel and saw her sitting by two other ladies. They all seemed to be having such a good time. I was glad for Aunt Mabel. She looked so pretty in that new dress. It was the only time I ever saw her in a dress.

I spent the rest of the evening in Eddy's room and some time after midnight, Cliff called me and the three of us drove home. By the time we pulled into Cliff's yard, Aunt Mabel and I were asleep. We stirred when Cliff beeped the horn of his Ford. We moaned and stepped from the truck and staggered toward his house.

"Come on in," he said as he lit a lantern. "Mabel, you can sleep on the couch and you," he pointed at me, "you know where your bed is."

I slept well but when I awoke, my butt and back hurt from the fall from Bernice's horse. When I came out of the bedroom I saw Cliff and Aunt Mabel having coffee.

"Did you sleep well," she asked as she ruffled her hair. Before I had a chance to answer, she continued, "And why are you walking as if ... you hurt yourself, didn't you?"

I looked at Cliff as he puffed on his pipe.

"And your pants are dirty and there's a tear in your knee. You didn't fall off one of their horses, did yah?"

"Well ... I didn't mean to but ..."

"Did you hurt yourself?"

"Not really, just a little sore."

"Anything else you need to tell me about last night?

"I ... kinda lost my hat in the darkness when Eddy started to race back to the farm. I did all I could to slow down the horse but when I rode ... "

"Did you win?" asked Cliff as his eyes twinkled.

"Winning a race on a run-away horse is ... you lost another hat?" Her voice became higher in pitch as she ended.

"I'll buy him one when I'm in town tomorrow. What size do you take?" asked Cliff as he relit his pipe.

Aunt Mabel closed her eyes and shook her head. "Oh well, I hope that you had a good time with Eddy and Bernice, They're well behaved."

"Do you want any cereal?" asked Cliff.

"In a minute but first I've got to go outside," I said.

When I stepped outside, the morning light was so bright that I shaded my eyes. After a few minutes, I walked around to the back of the house to the outhouse and was shocked at what I saw when I opened up the door. The seat was painted bright red. I couldn't believe my eyes. I started for the house to tell

Cliff and on the way I noticed something on the windmill. It looked like a pair of underwear.

I ran as I yelled. "**CLIFF! CLIFF!**"

He opened the door as I was coming up the steps.

"What the hell's the matter?" responded Cliff.

"The toilet seat in the outhouse has been painted red and there is a pair of underwear on your windmill," I said as I pointed for him to see.

"Oh, NO! Manny must have been here while we were sleeping. I'm afraid to see what my hogs look like."

He stirred the ashes in his pipe and dumped them on the ground. After repacking it with tobacco, he struck a match and lit it. Several puffs later he sat on the steps and started to laugh.

"It's a good thing that Manny only has one fortieth birthday," taunted Aunt Mabel as she sat down beside him.

"Yeah, I guess so but how in the world did Manny know?"

I pointed at Cliff's truck and there, down the entire side of his truck were hundreds of tiny red paint drops splashed everywhere.

"That may have given him a clue," teased Aunt Mabel. "And oh, look at your right elbow; you have red paint on it. Some criminals you two are."

The three of us toured the farmyard to see what other mischief Manny had done. Nothing else seemed to be disturbed.

"Where are Hoss and Tex?' asked Aunt Mabel.

"Don't know," said Cliff. "That's strange." Cliff puckered his lips and gave two long loud whistles. There was total silence and then I heard some barking that seemed to be coming from the barn.

I started to run toward to the barn. As I opened the door, I called "HOSS! TEX!"

Both dogs continued to bark so I entered the barn but they were not to be seen. Cliff whistled and called them again. Their barked sounded as if they were somewhere in a box.

Cliff grabbed the door leading to the hayloft and hurried up the stairs. When he opened the small door at the top of the stairs he was mobbed by Hoss and Tex.

"You know that Manny is a real gentleman. When he put the dogs in the hayloft, he also put a large pan of water for them to drink. That's why people like him," said Cliff as Hoss and Tex continued to lick his face.

We spent the entire afternoon trying to remove the paint from the side of Cliff's truck and I was glad that Cliff never did get angry about the tricks that had been played by Manny.

"It's true. If you spit into the wind; you get wet," is all Cliff said.

CHAPTER 18

A DIFFICULT ROAD

It was the last weekend of August and more hay had been cut. Some of it had been stacked into piles and some had been baled. A neighbor made an agreement with Aunt Mabel that he would do the work if he would receive half of the hay and bales. I did spend some time in the field watching him as he patiently drove his tractor in the hay field south of the house. When I returned to the yard, I took Donut for a long ride and … had tears when I removed the saddle. It seemed so unfair that I had to go home.

There had been several cool evenings and some light rain, which was a break from the hot weather. As we rode past the long row of trees, I noticed that the leaves had turned yellow overnight. The grasses had browned and several bushes at the front of Aunt Mabel's home had bright red leaves. Overhead, flocks of ducks and geese flew in a southerly direction in V formations. Even the crows had gathered and seemed restless. Gone were the wonderful songbirds that had met me every morning for autumn was now upon us.

Cliff commented on the change in the air. "It's different this morning. Fall is coming and nature is telling us that changes are on the way. I think I'll wear my sweater until noon," he said as he tapped the dead ashes from his pipe.

As the three of us sat on the hay wagon, Aunt Mabel handed sandwiches to us. They tasted so good. I never knew how good a beef sandwich could taste, especially when you had been working in the field.

"Well this weekend, we need to take you back to Three Hills 'cause your folks will be there to pick you up," Aunt Mabel said as she turned to reach into the food basket.

"Too bad you can't stay here with us," said Cliff as he tossed a piece of meat to Fritz.

"I hate to go home 'cause I've had such a good time." I turned my head to one side so that they could not see what was in my eyes. We ate in silence. Swallowing was difficult.

"Aunt Mabel, can I ask you a question?"

She tightened her lips and nodded, "Sure."

"Why do you live alone? I mean, if you knew that you would live on such a nice ranch, why not have kids?"

"Some questions are too personal to answer," interrupted Cliff as he tipped a cup of coffee to his lips.

"I was rather old when I married and then, well John died. All possibilities seemed to be gone." She paused to take a bite of her sandwich. After chewing a few moments, she resumed, "I wasn't sure that I would be a good mom."

"But that can't be true. Look how well you have treated me and what about the other nephews that you have had here? I'm sure they all had as good a time as me. I hate to say this, but I wish my mom was as nice as you."

She tried to hide her surprise and sadness but seemed pleased that I would say that.

I turned to Cliff, "And you, Cliff, you have been a neat friend. I mean that. You are kind and you've given me advice and even covered for me when I was ... was in trouble. You'd make a neat dad, if not a great uncle." Another tear found my cheek and then my chin. In silence I turned my sandwich over in my hand several times before raising it to my mouth.

Cliff removed his hat and blew the dust off it, adjusted the brim and placed it back on his head. "Thanks, kid, never had anyone say those kind things to me before. Let's get some more work done," he said gruffly, sounding uncomfortable with my compliments.

The afternoon was long but special because I realized that my time with them was limited. Soon I would be on my way home, on my way back to school and city life. I wiped several tears from my eyes and continued to wrestle with the bales of hay that Cliff had placed on the back of the truck.

After the Saturday evening meal, Aunt Mabel placed the dishes on the counter and sat down to enjoy her coffee. "Tomorrow, we have to take you back. Your parents will be in Three Hills, so I guess the summer vacation is over."

All of us sat in silence for a long time. Cliff sipped on his coffee as Aunt Mabel wiped her eyes with her apron. "Sure has been a great summer with you here," she said with a quiver in her voice

Later that evening, Cliff shook my hand before he went home. "If I had a son, I'd want him to be like you. You're tough, hard working and fun to be with. You can ride with me anytime."

As he and Aunt Mabel walked to his truck, I had to go

inside so he wouldn't see my tears. It was the first time that I felt hollow inside, as if something was being ripped out of me. I went to bed and lay in the darkness, wide awake, comparing myself to a prisoner who was to be executed the next morning. I relived every day and each experience, not wanting to forget anything. I remember the antique hall clock ringing two times before I found a comfortable position in that bed.

Sunday morning arrived and Aunt Mabel helped me pack all of my clothing. "I washed your clothes to save your mom extra work. It has been great to have you here. I hope you don't mind but I planned on going to church before we go to Aunt Annie's place."

"I don't want to go to the church with a diving board."

She chuckled, "Not the church camp but a real church. Do you mind?"

I was unable to speak and she seemed to understand that words were hard to form, so she hugged me for a long time. Eventually she walked away with her apron over her eyes.

We left at about nine a.m. and drove in silence. I was afraid to say what was on my mind. My stomach felt empty even though I had eaten. It was the most rotten feeling that I had ever felt.

As the Fargo moved out of the yard, I noticed the large stack of wood that needed to be split before winter. I wished I'd spent more time gathering and stacking wood. I wondered who would do it for her.

When the Fargo passed the grove of trees on my right, I could not help but notice the many bales that we had not loaded and brought to the barn. For a few moments, I felt sorry that I didn't do more for Aunt Mabel. Who would bring the bales into her yard and who would put them in the hayloft?

I looked back to see if I could see Fritz but we were too far down the road, besides my eyes were too … unable to see 'cause of tears. The last thing I remember seeing on the ranch was the sign post. Somehow it looked lonely and so I stared at it as we passed under it. I wanted to remember what that gateway with three large trees and a bony skull with one antler looked like.

When we passed under it, I looked back to see if I could see the broken antler but dust was swirling up behind the Fargo.

"You're very quiet. What's wrong?" she asked.

"I guess … I don't really know 'cause it seems that everything is ending so fast …"

She interrupted, "All is well. Sorrow and sadness is part of … part of growing up. Sometimes the hurt doesn't go away, regardless what you do. There is no position of comfort that will ease some disappointments."

"But I feel rotten inside, like … like I've lost my best friend and maybe …"

"Losing your best friend hurts more than this. Trust me, I know. You will always be in my heart and I know that Cliff will try to hide his …"

"But I like Cliff too and I think you like him too, so why don't you marry him? He would make a neat uncle."

There was a long pause and then she looked at me, "I trust you to keep a secret so don't disappoint me, OK?"

I nodded my head and my tears sealed our agreement.

"My life hasn't been easy. I got married and went to school to become a nurse. Two months after I graduated, I became a widow because of a car accident. His name was Aaron." She paused to wipe tears from her cheeks before continuing. "When the war broke out, I signed up and went to Europe to help the wounded in that terrible war and there I met and married a

British Air Force Officer. He died over Germany in a bombing raid. I ... never heard anything ... about him again."

"Whaaat was his name?" I asked in a whisper.

"George Donald Gardner."

A tear freely rolled down her cheeks and she slowed the Fargo to about thirty miles an hour. Unable to speak, I reached over to touch her arm as she shifted into third gear.

"When I returned to Canada, I needed a job, so I worked in the hospital in Red Deer. That's where I met John. He was a rancher and we moved to this ranch. He died when a black bull charged him. He was on horseback when the bull's horn caught his leg. It pulled him off the horse and he bled to death in the field. I found him late that evening and lay beside him all night even though I knew he was dead. My heart was beyond repair." She slowed the truck to about fifteen miles per hour as she reached for her handkerchief.

I didn't want to let Aunt Mabel see all of my tears so I sneaked the sleeve of my shirt across my eyes when she was not looking. After I cleared my throat I managed to say, "Cliff is such a neat guy. He doesn't cuss much and never smokes in the house and ... and he doesn't wear sox with holes in them and ... and he likes you and other people. What else could you want?" I didn't know what else to say, so I looked out the side window.

Several minutes passed and then I tried to change the subject so I asked, "Why did you call ... the ranch the Broken Antler Ranch?"

She drove for about a mile before she answered. "Tell you the truth, it was called Anderson's Broken Antler Ranch when John and I bought it but when John died, I changed it to the Broken Antler Ranch."

I turned and looked at her to see if she was telling the truth.

Not that I doubted her but somehow the name was something painful and I did not know it.

"There was a time when I almost changed it to the Broken Heart Ranch but Cliff came along ... and he ... he told me that he thought the name was not very good. So, I left it as the Broken Antler Ranch."

After a few minutes, she signaled and we turned into a small town, and stopped by a white church with a tall cross on a spire. As we walked up to the open door, I could hear the congregation singing a hymn. Suddenly I realized that I had missed going to church that summer.

As the offering plate moved down the pew, I reached into my pocket and took out a quarter. It wasn't much but I felt like I wanted to share it with God 'cause He had answered my prayer by not letting Aunt Mabel die ... and it was all that I had left. Just then my aunt handed me five dollars and motioned for me to put it into the plate, so I did.

Two ladies sang a duet and the minister stood up and read the story of the Prodigal Son. He emphasized the idea that there were three main characters in the story: the father, the older brother and the prodigal son. The prodigal deliberately did wrong and then admitted it. When he returned his father was willing to forgive him regardless of the bad he had done but the eldest son was angry, arrogant and unwilling to change. I remember the minister saying that God is like the father because He is willing to forgive all of the bad things that we may have done.

When the service was closed with prayer, I opened one eye and saw that Aunt Mabel had bowed her head and had closed her eyes.

Everyone was friendly and shook our hands at the door.

I enjoyed the sermon and was glad that we had come. Aunt Mabel didn't say much, and soon we were on the road to the town of Three Hills.

We drove in silence and after about a half hour, we slowed for the railroad track on the west side of town, only three blocks from Aunt Annie's house.

"Thanks for taking me to church. I never realized that a sermon could be that ... that neat," I said, hoping to break the silence in the truck.

"I guess that I need to think about what I've heard this morning," she said as we rounded the final corner and stopped in front of Aunt Annie's house. "If God can forgive the Prodigal Son, I suppose that He can forgive the prodigal daughter too."

She turned off the engine of the Fargo and I looked at my father's car. Unsure of what else to say, I rolled down the window. "Well, as I see it, God loves you. I like you and I know that Cliff likes you and ... well so does Fritz. Think about it. Two people and a dog care about you and ... God does too. Who else counts?"

She hugged me and cried. We walked up the sidewalk, hand in hand.

At the door of my Aunt Annie's house, I turned to her. "Aunt Mabel, thank you for the hat, the boots and the chance to ... grow up. I have my chaps and my gloves and ... and a New York Yankees cap."

She smiled.

"Please tell Cliff thanks for the new hat, but I won't need it in the city. You can have it so I'll leave it here.

"Yes you lost several hats and the one that survived your summer will be nailed to the post, next to the steps to my veranda. When I see that, I will remember how special you are."

Oswald called to me from across the street. I turned to see him running toward me. I was amazed how much he had grown.

Aunt Mabel's last words to me were, "Please come again. I know that Cliff and Fritz would like that very much and, I certainly would enjoy that too."

It was the best summer an eleven-year old city boy could have ever had.

CHAPTER 19

THE SOUND OF SILENCE

I never saw Aunt Mabel again. Illness caught up with her before I ever made it back to her ranch. When my mother told me about Aunt Mabel's death, sadness invaded my soul. The walk to school seemed farther than it had ever been before and it seemed that clouds covered the entire sky. In class, nothing that Miss Trentiuk spoke about made any sense, nor did I care.

At home, I sat in my room and looked at my blue and white chaps. I felt a deep emptiness inside. I would never forget my rides at the rodeos, the baseball game, the canoeing and the fishing trip. What about the days on the porch and the endless number of cookies? The most painful thing of all was, thinking about the day I said 'Goodbye,' not suspecting that it I would never see or speak to her again.

The smell of flowers bothers me for it reminds me of the day my family and I sat, in silence, looking at a shiny wooden casket. She was quite a person. She had been in Europe, served in the military as a nurse, owned a ranch and was free to live as she pleased but now her true freedom was her freedom from pain.

I looked in every pew of the church for Cliff, but did not see him. How could he not come? My anxiety was curbed only by the thought that he may have been too heartbroken to attend or maybe he thought he would not be welcomed by the family.

The silence in the room was so strong that I could reach out and touch it. It reminded me of my first night in Aunt Mabel's house. It was a night of fear and uncertainty just as this day was.

The organ began to play and my mother began to cry. Everyone said that it was a very nice funeral, if there is such a thing, but I don't remember much of the service because I spent most of my time looking for Cliff. When lunch was served, I saw Manny Cunningham and Trigve Gunderson but I didn't speak to them. Later, I regretted my decision to avoid them but my chest hurt too much.

She was an aunt that referred to herself as the 'Prodigal Daughter' but how could God not forgive her? Did she suffer more before she died? Who really knew?

These years of silence have haunted me and now too much time has passed for me to look for her ranch. And what happened to Fritz? Who took care of him? And Cliff, by now, he must be an old man, if he's still alive.

Every kid should have an Aunt Mabel, a friend like Cliff and a summer as I did. I never really saw the end coming.

EPILOGUE

Time has a way of insidiously putting dust onto my memory and now that I have time to look at old photographs given to me by my aged mother, my emotions prompt me to ask about family truths that have, for years, seemed unimportant or non-existent. Silent faces stare at me from small black and white photographs and these faces leave me with the impression that they would like an opportunity to spend time with me and tell secrets which I neither knew nor suspected. Years have passed since they left us with tears on our cheeks and aches in our hearts, yet their gazes call to me, in a strange and disquieting way.

The sternness in my father's eyes in the photos seemed to have changed, for now they seem eager to wish me luck, to encourage and to tell me that I turned out OK. Uncles and aunts stand beside old cars, stimulating memories of plates of sandwiches, chocolate cake, noodle soup, Black Jack gum and scratchy records being played in parlors with cold linoleum flooring. Pictures of Christmas trees with only half the bulbs working, presents with weird colored paper, and forgotten family members prompt me to reminisce.

Three photographs exist of Aunt Mabel. One photograph

shows her standing next to an old windmill when her family lived on the prairies, one where she is wearing a fancy hat, and one faded, partially destroyed photograph of her wearing a military uniform, a wedge hat and stripes on her uniform jacket. She appears so healthy, so eager to serve and so ready for whatever life plans to toss at her. After moments of blurred vision, I turned it over to read what someone had printed in pencil above the date, 1943.

"Three medals for bravery, one year in POW, Medical Discharge."

After reading this message again and again, I am convinced that this is not the aunt I knew. Only my mother could shed light on this photograph that seemed to be intentionally placed near the bottom of the cardboard box that once held chocolates.

Unable to recall what the medals were for or where they might be, my mother narrowed her brows as she looked at the photograph. After moments of silence, she wiped a tear from her eyes and said, "She challenged everything and everyone. If there were an easy way to do something, she would try a new and different way. She had this idea that she was invincible and believed that those who followed rules had no grit." After dabbing her eyes with tissue she continued, "We found it hard to believe her stories about being in a room with Churchill and of knowing people in the French Underground." She sighed and looked away, "I guess we were too small for her."

A few moments later, she handed the pictures back to me and remained silent. Finally she raised her head and said, "We all loved her but she seemed to be a disappointment to mom and especially dad. Somewhere along the way, they decided to ignore her. Now that I think about it, she must have been hurt by that." A moment later she wiped another tear from her eye before continuing, "She was the eldest and looked different from us, curly hair and all. Now that I've looked at her picture again, she reminds me of a picture I once saw of dad's oldest brother, Uncle Earl."

"Did I ever meet him?"

"Oh no, I never saw him either," she said as she adjusted her glasses on her nose. We were told that he died when he was about twenty-one but I don't remember what he died from." She hesitated as she scratched at the remaining black and white photos in the bottom of the cardboard box. "I don't think we have a picture of Uncle Earl. Mom had one but I couldn't guess where it is or what became of it."

After putting all of the photographs back into the old chocolate box and placing it in my mother's dresser drawer, I put Aunt Mabel's photograph in my shirt pocket.

Her memory prompted me to sit silently in my home and remember. Several hours later when it was dark, I drove out of town to an isolated field and lay on the ground to look at the stars. It was true what Aunt Mabel said my first night on her ranch; the darkest sky shows the brightest stars.

When I arrived at home about midnight, I placed Aunt Mabel's photograph on the mirror of my dresser before lying down to a restless sleep. There was so much to remember and yet so much to regret.

Her photograph remains on that mirror and every morning I rise to face another day, I look at it. She is my daily inspiration.

What I wouldn't give to be with her for an hour, even if it were not on the Broken Antler Ranch.

www.ingramcontent.com/pod-product-compliance
Lightning Source LLC
Chambersburg PA
CBHW021625120626
46545CB00002B/399